My Memories of Śrīla Prabhupāda

Books Authored by Bhakti Vikāsa Swami

A Beginner's Guide to Kṛṣṇa Consciousness

A Message to the Youth of India

Brahmacarya in Kṛṣṇa Consciousness

Glimpses of Traditional Indian Life

Jaya Śrīla Prabhupāda!

My Memories of Śrīla Prabhupāda

On Pilgrimage in Holy India

On Speaking Strongly in Śrīla Prabhupāda's Service

Patropadeśa

Śrī Bhaktisiddhānta Vaibhava (three volumes)

Śrī Caitanya Mahāprabhu

Śrī Vaṁśīdāsa Bābājī

Vaiṣṇava Śikhā o Sādhana (Bengali)

Women: Masters or Mothers?

Books Edited or Compiled by Bhakti Vikāsa Swami

Rāmāyaṇa

The Story of Rasikānanda

Gauḍīya Vaiṣṇava Padyāvalī (Bengali)

Śrī Śrī Guru-Gaurāṅgau Jayataḥ

My Memories of Śrīla Prabhupāda

and other writings

Second Edition
(Revised and Enlarged)

Bhakti Vikāsa Swami

ISBN 978-93-82109-30-3

www.bvks.com
books@bvks.com

Previous printings: 4,000 copies

Second Edition (2012): 3,000 copies

Published by Bhakti Vikas Trust, Surat, India
Printed by Lightning Source

Dedication

Offered, as Gaṅgā is offered to Gaṅgā, to the lotus feet of His Divine Grace A.C. Bhaktivedanta Swami Prabhupāda, the founder-*ācārya* of the International Society for Krishna Consciousness, the foremost devotee of the modern age, the spiritual master of the entire universe, and my personal savior and ever well-wisher.

Contents

Legend
Cc—*Śrī Caitanya-caritāmṛta*
SB—*Śrīmad-Bhāgavatam*

Preface to the Second Edition

In this edition, a few extra details have been added to the biographical portion, and an error corrected: in one anecdote I had named Nanda-kumāra Dāsa as the devotee who wore *japa* beads round his neck, but according to other devotees who were present, he was not in England at that time *(see p. 8)*. Also, the section featuring Vyāsa-*pūjā* offerings has been enlarged and now includes all the homages that I have written to date. Vyāsa-*pūjā* offerings have been included largely as they appeared. The essay "On Speaking Strongly in Śrīla Prabhupāda's Service" has been omitted (it has been published as a separate book).

Introduction

I joined ISKCON in 1975, when Śrīla Prabhupāda was already established as a great world *ācārya* and had several thousand disciples. By that time, only a few devotees were allowed regular personal access to Śrīla Prabhupāda; the rest were discouraged from disturbing him. Even while traveling and preaching extensively, Śrīla Prabhupāda set aside as much time as possible for his foremost work: translating books. We were told that more important than seeing Śrīla Prabhupāda in person (*vapuḥ*) is to follow his instructions (*vāṇī*), and that he was especially pleased by distribution of his books. (In those days, most of the *brahmacārīs* were engaged in that service.) Of course, we got to see Śrīla Prabhupāda in classes and *darśanas*, during which he freely gave his personal association to everyone.

Although I saw Śrīla Prabhupāda several times before he passed away (on 14 November 1977), only once was I ever alone in a room with him—when he gave me the Gāyatrī mantra. It may be questioned why one with so few memories of Śrīla Prabhupāda would bother to publish them. The first reason is that many newer devotees ask me about my experiences with Śrīla Prabhupāda, and I wish to share whatever little I can tell with those who are eager to hear. Furthermore, while my personal anecdotes regarding Śrīla Prabhupāda naturally have special meaning for me, they are also significant for the entire world, because everything that Śrīla Prabhupāda said or did is important for everyone and hence should be recorded and preserved, as far as possible. So another reason for my publishing these few vignettes is to encourage others to write or otherwise record theirs. Many disciples had extensive association with Śrīla Prabhupāda, others had less, and still others (as in my case) had very little. But if many of the devotees with only a few remembrances were to publish them, the world would then have a vast treasure of informative, instructive, and enlivening narratives—a significant record for posterity.

In the early days of ISKCON most devotees were absorbed in a variety of services, and record-keeping was practically the last thing on anyone's mind. (Hari Śauri Prabhu, having the foresight to keep notes, was an exception. No one else possesses such extensive, coherent, and historically reliable records of their association with Śrīla Prabhupāda.) Therefore, in recalling the following incidents twenty years after they occurred, despite attempting to retain historical and chronological accuracy, I must admit that within my mind the particulars of Śrīla Prabhupāda's visits to England in 1975 and 1976 have become conflated, and hence these accounts may be considered a personal meditation rather than authoritative history.

In this book I have also included some thoughts and realizations about Śrīla Prabhupāda and his movement, as well as all the Vyāsa-*pūjā* homages I have written to date.

All glories to His Divine Grace Śrīla Prabhupāda!

KRSNA
KRSNA
Bhagavad-gita
As It Is

The Pāṇḍavas were so dear to Kṛṣṇa. So it is better to hear about the Pāṇḍavas than to hear about Kṛṣṇa. People may be very much inclined to hear about Kṛṣṇa, but the *śāstra* says, "To hear about the devotees of Kṛṣṇa is still better."

Śrīla Prabhupāda (Lecture—28 December 1973)

My Memories of Śrīla Prabhupāda

I first met Śrīla Prabhupāda in Ireland, early in 1975, in the form of one of his books—a paperback edition of *Kṛṣṇa, the Supreme Personality of Godhead* (Volume Two). The sky-blue cover featured a beautiful silver-framed picture of Kṛṣṇa and Balarāma, and the back cover displayed an equally attractive photograph of Śrīla Prabhupāda. I read from the beginning of the book (it started at Chapter Thirty-six), the first three sentences of which remain in my mind even now:

> Vṛndāvana was always absorbed in the thought of Kṛṣṇa. Everyone remembered His pastimes and was constantly merged in the ocean of transcendental bliss. But the material world is so contaminated that even in Vṛndāvana the *asuras* or demons tried to disturb the peaceful situation.

Although eager to read the book, I progressed through it slowly, as I found the content to be weighty and recondite, and the linguistic style and the many Indian words unusual. Yet I recognized that the message was from a platform beyond the triviality of this world, and I began to follow, at least in a small way, one instruction that Śrīla Prabhupāda has given therein—to chant the Hare Kṛṣṇa mantra. I continued to read, with no idea about the significance of what I was doing. Little did I know that soon my frustration, emptiness, and misery would be finished forever, and that—with shaved head, Vaiṣṇava *tilaka*, orange robes, a beadbag, and a big smile—I myself would distribute thousands of such books.

About two years earlier, my best friend at school had bought some books from devotees on Oxford Street, London. He wanted to show them to me, but I didn't even want to see them, and scoffed, "All these Indian swamis are cheaters." But by this time I was more receptive, and after reading *Kṛṣṇa* I decided to visit the devotees. Thus, my next acquaintance with Śrīla Prabhupāda was in the form of his devotees and his movement. And in April 1975, I was fortunate enough to be accepted into the community of devotees at Bhaktivedanta Manor, near London.

The devotees often spoke about Śrīla Prabhupāda, with great reverence, faith, and affection. They would teach me the philosophy and practices of Kṛṣṇa consciousness by saying, "Śrīla Prabhupāda said this" or "He showed us to do like that." And they constantly reveled in discussing Śrīla Prabhupāda's wonderful activities as he traversed the globe like a transcendental world conqueror. Much of our news about His Divine Grace was relayed by devotees passing through London. (Śrīla Prabhupāda had discouraged unnecessary international phone calling, and the internet was yet to be.) We would eagerly gather round a visiting devotee to relish hearing about the exciting things Śrīla Prabhupāda had said—maybe chastisement for some, encouraging words for others, a new revelation from his recent translations, or his latest plans for spreading Kṛṣṇa consciousness.

Whether within the temple or out traveling in *saṅkīrtana* vans, devotees regularly listened to cassettes of Śrīla Prabhupāda speaking and chanting. We were saturated with Prabhupāda consciousness. Even though I knew little of what it means to be a disciple, I was worshiping Śrīla Prabhupāda as my guru.

In the summer of 1975, news came that Śrīla Prabhupāda was in Paris and would soon come to London. Just by hearing this, the devotees in Britain became joyful, and as the moment of His Divine Grace's expected arrival drew nearer, a mood of tremendous excitement spread among them. At Bhaktivedanta Manor, devotees were busy cleaning, painting, and putting everything in order. On 11 August, almost all of us went to receive Śrīla Prabhupāda at Heathrow Airport. We were happily performing *kīrtana,* in great anticipation of seeing our beloved spiritual master—and then were informed that his trip to London had been cancelled! Our intense disappointment was soon replaced by renewed expectancy when we were further told that Śrīla Prabhupāda was rescheduled to arrive just one day later.

Next day at the airport, there was some confusion as to which terminal Śrīla Prabhupāda would be arriving at. Most of the devotees did greet Śrīla Prabhupāda upon his arrival, but I ended up in a smaller group at another terminal. We were joyfully chanting when all of a sudden Harikeśa Dāsa Brahmacārī rushed up and with a blissful smile told us that we were at the wrong terminal, and that Śrīla Prabhupāda had already arrived and left for the Manor. (Because there had been some mix-up regarding Śrīla Prabhupāda's baggage, Harikeśa Prabhu had stayed back to retrieve it.) Our plan had been to greet Śrīla Prabhupāda with *kīrtana* at the airport and then rush ahead to again greet him with *kīrtana* at the Manor. So we immediately piled into the vans and sped back—but too late! Śrīla Prabhupāda was already in his quarters and would not emerge until the next morning. Until then, all but a few senior devotees would have to wait for Śrīla Prabhupāda's *darśana.*

I first saw Śrīla Prabhupāda the next morning, 13 Aug 1975, shortly before the scheduled *darśana* of the Deities at 7:15 a.m. Flanked by Brahmānanda Swami, Harikeśa Prabhu, and other big-bodied American devotees, next to whom the slightness of Śrīla Prabhupāda's physical stature was accentuated, Śrīla Prabhupāda majestically descended the stairs. And thus my first impression upon directly seeing my eternal lord and master was rather mundane: I was surprised to see how short

Śrīla Prabhupāda was. (Having heard him speak so powerfully on tapes and seen his aristocratic demeanor in photos, I had presumed Śrīla Prabhupāda to be tall and well built.) But that initial impression lasted only a moment, for I was able to adjust my thoughts and remember that a great spiritual personality is not to be judged by external criteria.

The devotees were so awed by Śrīla Prabhupāda's presence that the atmosphere was grave and slightly tense. Śrīla Prabhupāda also appeared grave, but his gravity seemed greater than that of the entire assembly of devotees. (In retrospect, I had never before experienced such a deep collective mood, even though previously, as a Catholic altar boy, I had attended many funerals.)

Upon seeing Śrīla Prabhupāda at the top of the staircase, all the devotees waiting outside the temple room immediately bowed down—all except me. I thought, "Let me *see* Śrīla Prabhupāda." Śrīla Prabhupāda appeared effulgent, and more grave than anyone I had ever seen before. I simply stared at his divine form and wanted to continue, but knowing and feeling it to be improper not to bow down, after a few seconds I also offered obeisance.

When I arose, I saw that Śrīla Prabhupāda had reached the door of the temple. He then lifted his lotus feet one after the other to allow his slippers to be removed by a fortunate devotee. I was surprised, for I had never seen or heard of such a practice. As a newcomer, I was regularly being surprised to learn of customs that I had not seen or heard of before, and this was one more, which I took mental note of: the spiritual master's slippers are removed by a disciple.

Along with the many others following behind Śrīla Prabhupāda, I squeezed through the door into the packed temple room.

As Śrīla Prabhupāda entered, the lively *kīrtana* that had been going on suddenly stopped. Although some devotees appeared joyful, most looked reverential or even apprehensive. Through a lane of devotees bowing on both sides, Śrīla Prabhupāda regally strode toward the altar.

Again, I stood and watched for a few extra moments while everyone else prostrated. I wanted to see what Śrīla Prabhupāda would do. I was watching him from behind as he walked the length of the temple room. His palms joined, he stood for some seconds before the presiding Deities Śrī Śrī Rādhā-Gokulānanda and then offered full obeisance. The devotees, who by this time had risen from prostrating and were now intently watching Śrīla Prabhupāda, again offered obeisance along with their spiritual master. Śrīla Prabhupāda then took *darśana* of Their Lordships and was given *caraṇāmṛta.*

Proceeding to the opposite end of the temple, Śrīla Prabhupāda sat upon the magnificent, elevated *vyāsāsana* and accepted guru-*pūjā*. After chanting "Jaya Rādhā Mādhava," he gazed silently for several minutes at the Deities. He then spoke feelingly about the beauty of Kṛṣṇa, and proceeded to lecture on *Śrīmad-Bhāgavatam* (6.1.55).

The next morning, 14 August, Śrīla Prabhupāda departed for Bombay.

During that visit to the Manor, Śrīla Prabhupāda accepted several new candidates as aspirants for initiation, including me. And on the following Janmāṣṭamī, on Śrīla Prabhupāda's behalf, Haṁsadūta Prabhu (our GBC representative) conducted an initiation ceremony. At that time, I received the name Ilāpati Dāsa Brahmacārī.

Śrīla Prabhupāda next visited England between 21 and 28 July 1976. He arrived with a heavy cold, and rested more than usual.

Nevertheless, as was typical for Śrīla Prabhupāda, his visit was marked with several significant events. I was a fledgling member of the devotee community, so was not invited to participate in or attend those events, but simply heard about them afterward from senior devotees. I was rather impressed that Śrīla Prabhupāda had given an interview to a journalist from the highbrow *Observer* newspaper, but less so on hearing that George Harrison was coming to meet Śrīla Prabhupāda. I had no interest in music icons and considered that the enthusiasm some devotees had for George was simply a hangover from their pre-devotional lives. In fact, when a certain devotee excitedly informed some of us of George's arrival, it seemed that he expected us to join him in rushing to try to catch a glimpse of that great star—so I deliberately went in another direction. I might have better respected George had I known how much affection Śrīla Prabhupāda had for him.

During this visit by Śrīla Prabhupāda, I was able to go on a morning walk with him—the only one I ever attended. About thirty devotees were present, since most of the others had been uninformed of the walk or told not to attend, to prevent too large a crowd. When several others and myself unexpectedly saw Śrīla Prabhupāda leaving the Manor, we scrambled to follow, but Bhaja Hari Prabhu, who had been the temple president until just recently, forbade us. However, when I noticed a godbrother going along anyway, I did too, and no one objected. During this walk, Śrīla Prabhupāda hardly spoke, apart from his continuous chanting of *japa*, in which the accompanying devotees joined him. I was at the back of the group, just trying to get a glimpse of Śrīla Prabhupāda. Since he was surrounded by many senior devotees, I couldn't hear anything he said.

I attended both of the public *darśanas* that Śrīla Prabhupāda gave during that visit, by squeezing into the largest room of his quarters with about a hundred other eager godsiblings.

During the first of those *darśanas*, a devotee was sitting in front and slightly to the right of Śrīla Prabhupāda and chanting. His *japa* beads were around his neck and he was holding them with both hands. Śrīla Prabhupāda had been answering some questions but suddenly turned and asked, "Where is your bead bag?" The disciple replied, "It is being washed, Śrīla Prabhupāda." Then, indicating the adjacent bedroom, Śrīla Prabhupāda asked Harikeśa Mahārāja (he had been awarded *sannyāsa* within the past year), "Some bead bags have been given?" in a manner that questioned Harikeśa Mahārāja's knowledge or remembrance of it. Upon Mahārāja's reply in the affirmative, Śrīla Prabhupāda said, "Give one to him" and told that devotee, "You should keep two bead bags. Always chant with your beads in your bead bag. When one is being washed, use the other one."

When a young Indian couple came in, Śrīla Prabhupāda interrupted his speaking to disciples and instead addressed these visitors. I do not recall what he said to them, but I remember how Śrīla Prabhupāda changed his tone and demeanor from that of a dispenser of absolute knowledge to a welcoming fatherly host. The couple stayed briefly. Apparently they wanted only literal *darśana*—just to see Śrīla Prabhupāda but not hear him. As they left, Śrīla Prabhupāda instructed, "Give them some *prasāda*." I was struck by Śrīla Prabhupāda's concern that they receive *prasāda*.

The second *darśana*, on 27 July, comprised an interview with Mike Robinson of the London Broadcasting Corporation, a local radio station.* Devotees were already crowding the room when Mr. Robinson entered. Mukunda Prabhu, who had organized the meeting, asked Mr. Robinson if he wanted the devotees to

* This interview appears as the chapter "Reincarnation and Beyond" in *The Science of Self-Realization*.

leave during the interview.* But Mr. Robinson did not want to inconvenience anyone, so even though Mukunda Prabhu asked him twice, he insisted that it was alright for everyone to stay. Then Śrīla Prabhupāda, seated upon his *āsana*, looked up at the standing Mukunda Prabhu to inquire what was being discussed. When Mukunda Prabhu explained, Śrīla Prabhupāda shook his head sideways in the typical Indian gesture of acquiescence.

Mr. Robinson was very respectful to Śrīla Prabhupāda. Twice Śrīla Prabhupāda asked him to sit on a chair, but Mr. Robinson insisted to remain sitting on the floor before Śrīla Prabhupāda. He spoke to Śrīla Prabhupāda with the submissiveness of a disciple. Śrīla Prabhupāda reciprocated by speaking to him strongly and firmly, but with patience, as if instructing a child. Mike Robinson was there to ask questions, but Śrīla Prabhupāda was in command of the proceedings.

During the interview, I became surprised to see the intimacy of Śrīla Prabhupāda's dealings with Mukunda Prabhu. I did not know much about the history of the movement or the significant role Mukunda Prabhu had played, nor how close he was to Śrīla Prabhupāda. Because Mukunda Prabhu was always humble and unassuming, I had not realized how important and spiritually advanced he was.

During one *darśana*, Śrīla Prabhupāda's glance fell upon me, and I was bold enough to hold it. Śrīla Prabhupāda did not exactly look *at* me, but *into* me. I felt ashamed for all the nasty things he was seeing. Śrīla Prabhupāda's glance also expressed concern. His eyes rested on me for just a moment and then turned elsewhere.

---

* Mukunda Prabhu later accepted *sannyāsa*, and is now known as Mukunda Goswami.

At the end of one *darśana,* I gave a little gift to Śrīla Prabhupāda. I had noticed that many devotees were presenting him gifts and had read in *The Nectar of Devotion* that one should offer to the Deity something that is dear to himself. Besides minimal clothing and toiletries, I barely had any possessions. But I happened to have a small unframed photo of Londonīśvara, the Kṛṣṇa Deity in our temple in central London, and it was dear to me. So I decided to give it to Śrīla Prabhupāda. Actually, I should have framed and nicely wrapped it, but I did not know such things. Nor did I, a *brahmacārī,* have any personal money. (In those days, for a *brahmacārī* to have his own money, even for buying a gift for Śrīla Prabhupāda, was considered improper.) Devotees were standing in line at the end of the *darśana* room to offer obeisance to Śrīla Prabhupāda. A devotee ahead of me offered a flower. When I approached, I gave the photo and paid obeisance. I hoped that Śrīla Prabhupāda would acknowledge my gift, but he simply touched it to his head without saying anything.

On 25 July, Śrīla Prabhupāda visited the temple of Śrī Śrī Rādhā-Londonīśvara at Bury Place, in central London. On the way back to the Manor, he stopped at the home of his disciple Kṣīrodakaśāyī Viṣṇu Prabhu, in North London. News of this outing was deliberately withheld from most of the devotees, since both venues were too small to accommodate many persons. I learned about that event at the last minute, and although I did not care about the stern warning not to go, I had no means to do so. All the vehicles were full and I had no money for a taxi to the tube station.

After Śrīla Prabhupāda returned from central London, I heard that he had approved the purchase of a building in a prime location just off Oxford Street as the new abode of Śrī Śrī Rādhā-Londonīśvara. This was another significant step forward for ISKCON in England that marked the administration of our new GBC man, Jayatīrtha Prabhu, who in less than four months had given new direction and dynamism to the movement in England while himself remaining the model of a soft-spoken, unassuming Vaiṣṇava. This London acquisition was but one of several outstanding properties worldwide that Śrīla Prabhupāda and his disciples had secured in the previous two to three years. So my excitation upon hearing of it was tempered by a sense of matter-of-factness in knowing that for Śrīla Prabhupāda the extraordinary was commonplace.

My subsequent memories of Śrīla Prabhupāda are of him in India, during the Māyāpur-Vṛndāvana festival of 1976.

While on the plane to Delhi, I started to feel drowsy and nauseous. When after my arrival the symptoms persisted, I consulted a doctor. To my dismay, it was not a simple case of travel sickness—I had hepatitis! Shortly before, a devotee had arrived at Bhaktivedanta Manor from Africa with hepatitis, so I must have contracted it from him. Especially during the first portion of the festival, in Māyāpur, I was very drowsy and weak.

I was inconceivably fortunate to be in Māyāpur with so many devotees from all over the world who were exuberantly performing immense *kīrtanas* and daily seeing and hearing from Śrīla Prabhupāda. (Just one year before, I had no knowledge about any of this.) Yet I was so sick that I could barely stand, and thus I could not properly avail of the opportunity. Still, I did manage to attend all of Śrīla Prabhupāda's lectures, even though I struggled to remain awake during them.

Śrīla Prabhupāda was lecturing on the prayers of Prahlāda Mahārāja to Nṛsiṁhadeva, in *Śrīmad-Bhāgavatam*, Seventh Canto, which Śrīla Prabhupāda was translating at that time. That this section had not yet been published and thus was unknown to most of the devotees, increased their excitement and eagerness to hear it.

Just as Prahlāda Mahārāja had done, Śrīla Prabhupāda spoke strongly, fearlessly, and with full realization, intricately analyzing the position of the material world and scything away at all *anarthas.* The temple room was filled with blissful and enthusiastic devotees. During the lecture, whenever Śrīla Prabhupāda chanted the Hare Kṛṣṇa *mahā-mantra* or the "*harer nāma, harer nāma*" verse, all the devotees would chant jubilantly along with him.

Throughout these classes, Haṁsadūta Prabhu would stand behind and to the left of Śrīla Prabhupāda, whisking him with a *cāmara,* and other leaders, such as Puṣṭa Kṛṣṇa Swami and Brahmānanda Swami, would stand around the *vyāsāsana.* Śrīla Prabhupāda looked like an emperor surrounded by his ministers.

At the beginning of the class given on 11 March, after chanting the Sanskrit *śloka* responsively with the devotees, Śrīla Prabhupāda exhorted all to individually chant the Sanskrit verse. I felt pleased and encouraged by that, because I always enjoyed chanting the verse in classes. Later in that lecture Śrīla Prabhupāda said, "I am very glad that you European and American boys have taken so much trouble to come here"—which made me feel happy. He continued, "But you'll be benefited if you come here and try to take lessons from Caitanya Mahāprabhu as He taught Sanātana Gosvāmī." I inferred that Śrīla Prabhupāda was cautioning us not to misuse our time or act frivolously while in Māyāpur. I also wondered how we could go about taking lessons from Caitanya Mahāprabhu. Although I did not immediately realize the answer, sometime in the future it became apparent to me that to hear from Śrīla Prabhupāda is as good as hearing from Lord Caitanya.

In his lecture of 13 March, Śrīla Prabhupāda stressed how the material world is so contaminated that even Lord Brahmā had to purify himself by undergoing austerities for many hundreds of years, and even though we are very, very fallen compared to Brahmā, Lord Caitanya is so kind that He nonetheless gives us a "little formula":

हरेर्नाम हरेर्नाम हरेर्नामैव केवलम् ।
कलौ नास्त्येव नास्त्येव नास्त्येव गतिरन्यथा ॥

harer nāma harer nāma harer nāmaiva kevalam
kalau nāsty eva nāsty eva nāsty eva gatir anyathā

On Gaura-*pūrṇimā,* toward the end of his lecture Śrīla Prabhupāda said, "Don't forget that Śrī Caitanya Mahāprabhu is the Supreme Personality of Godhead." I became surprised, wondering, "How could we possibly forget that Śrī Caitanya Mahāprabhu is the Supreme Personality of Godhead?" A few minutes later, I was awakened from hepatitic drowsiness by the devotees joining Śrīla Prabhupāda in chanting *śrī-kṛṣṇa-caitanya prabhu nityānanda śrī-advaita gadādhara śrīvāsādi-gaura-bhakta-vṛnda.* After that, Śrīla Prabhupāda said, "This will make your life perfect. Thank you very much," ending the lecture to a great roar of appreciation.

On 18 March, two days after Gaura-*pūrṇimā,* in his *Bhāgavatam* lecture Śrīla Prabhupāda said, "*Śrīmad-Bhāgavatam* should be your life and soul, to remain constantly in Kṛṣṇa consciousness." This instruction became an important focus in my life. I considered the meaning of "*Śrīmad-Bhāgavatam* should be your life and soul." And still today, when lecturing or otherwise preaching to devotees, I often quote this instruction and elaborate on its meaning—that we should regularly read *Śrīmad-Bhāgavatam,* meditate on its content, memorize its principal *ślokas,* discuss it among devotees, and distribute it widely. We must conduct our lives according to the instructions of *Śrīmad-Bhāgavatam* and thus become servants of the *Bhāgavatam* and of the *mahā-mahā-bhāgavata* who has given us the *Bhāgavatam*.

One evening, while sauntering without any particular purpose or direction along the second-floor veranda of the original building of ISKCON Māyāpur, I came upon Śrīla Prabhupāda's *darśana* room. Devotees were tightly gathered at the entrance, and laughter issued from within. Peeking over the shoulders of devotees at the window, I saw that Śrīla Prabhupāda was giving *darśana*. "Why am I missing this?" I thought. "Why didn't I know about this?" I looked at the devotees packed into the room—no "big shots." It was an open, general *darśana*. I thought, "Here's my chance. I could be in there just as well as anyone else." Although there seemed to be no way to enter, somehow I squeezed in and even managed (with the "nothing's impossible" spirit of a *saṅkīrtana* devotee) to get a squashed sitting place in front of Śrīla Prabhupāda's table. I do not recall what was discussed, just that Śrīla Prabhupāda was leaning on his bolster, sitting with one knee in the air, relaxed, smiling, and joking, happy to be with his disciples. The devotees were mostly rank-and-filers like myself, who generally served Śrīla Prabhupāda from a distance, with little prospect of attaining his personal association. They were all clearly delighted to have this chance to be with their spiritual master—as I also was.

After I had been in the room for a few minutes, Ānakadundubhi Prabhu, a lanky British *pūjārī*, appeared at the door, holding a large plate of *mahā-prasāda* fruit. Seeing little opportunity for entering, he just stood there. After a short time, Śrīla Prabhupāda noticed Ānakadundubhi Prabhu and told him to distribute the *prasāda* to the devotees. Ānakadundubhi Prabhu replied, "I was going to give it to them when they leave." Śrīla Prabhupāda immediately quipped, "They will never leave." The

devotees laughed and cheered "*Jaya* Śrīla Prabhupāda!" Śrīla Prabhupāda then indicated to Ānakadundubhi Prabhu to come inside, which he somehow or other did. Śrīla Prabhupāda took a piece of the fruit, and Ānakadundubhi Prabhu stood ready to distribute the remainder, which served as a cue for the devotees to stand up, take a little *prasāda,* and leave.

Afterward, I thought about those words: "They will never leave." Although stated jokingly, it was true—deeply true. The devotees were so intensely bound to Śrīla Prabhupāda in love that they could never leave him. Even if, being overwhelmed by *māyā,* they were to leave him temporarily, they could never forget Śrīla Prabhupāda's lotus feet or his kindness upon them.

The festival then moved on to Vṛndāvana, where Śrīla Prabhupāda continued lecturing on the Seventh Canto. There I heard that Harikeśa Mahārāja had noted that while undertaking the translation of the section describing Prahlāda Mahārāja, Śrīla Prabhupāda had become deeply absorbed in the mood of Prahlāda Mahārāja. Just like Prahlāda Mahārāja, Śrīla Prabhupāda had exhibited extraordinary compassion toward the fallen living beings, simply considering how to save them, and being more concerned with serving his spiritual master than enjoying the happiness of associating with Kṛṣṇa.

A few days before, during a class in Māyāpur, Śrīla Prabhupāda had explained that an affectionate mother feels her child's pain even more than does the child himself. Reflecting the mood of Prahlāda Mahārāja—about whom all of those *Bhāgavatam* verses under discussion had been written—Śrīla Prabhupāda felt great pain at the suffering of all conditioned souls. Therefore he worked tirelessly on those translations, to help save all living entities from repeated birth and death.

As in Māyāpur, so also in Vṛndāvana the temple room was always packed during classes. Śrīla Prabhupāda would sing "Jaya

Rādhā Mādhava," shaking his head in great absorption as he chanted in his incomparable way. Nitāicānd Dāsa Brahmacārī, young, trim, and looking quite grand, would stand to Śrīla Prabhupāda's right, intricately beating the *mṛdaṅga*. One morning, Śrīla Prabhupāda recounted an incident he had seen in Calcutta of a man who had half-killed a chicken by slitting its throat. Dying in pain, the chicken was squawking and jumping about. Although his son was crying, the man was laughing and asking, "Why are you crying? It is very nice." Then Śrīla Prabhupāda said, "Just see. Without being a devotee, a man will become cruel, cruel, cruel, cruel, cruel—in this way go to hell." Śrīla Prabhupāda repeated the word *cruel* with great feeling.

I was shocked at how directly and forcefully Śrīla Prabhupāda spoke while lecturing on *Śrīmad-Bhāgavatam* 7.9.47, on 2 April 1976. He explained that it is not possible to imitate great devotees like Haridāsa Ṭhākura by going off to chant in solitude, and stressed that we must remain active in devotional service under the direction of authorities, and that by doing so we would realize Kṛṣṇa. Śrīla Prabhupāda particularly mentioned book distribution. As far as I remember, on this day the devotees were scheduled to go to Rādhā-kuṇḍa. (The devotees would travel each day by bus to different hallowed sites in Vraja-*maṇḍala*. Senior devotees who were familiar with Vṛndāvana would speak about the respective places and read from Śrīla Prabhupāda's books on the pastimes connected to each site.) It struck me that on this particular morning Śrīla Prabhupāda gave a stern warning regarding Rādhā-kuṇḍa.

After the class, I heard that Śrīla Prabhupāda had strongly admonished devotees not to be lured into imitative *bābājī* life: "Don't think you can simply sit in one place and chant. You will simply eat and sleep, think of women and money, and fall down. There are already so many monkeys, hogs, and dogs in

Vṛndāvana. Do not become another one of them. Do not act like a monkey. Don't try to jump over your spiritual master."*

One morning just after seven o'clock, I happened to see Śrīla Prabhupāda enter the temple compound as he was returning from a walk with a group of about fifteen leading disciples. As Śrīla Prabhupāda strode toward the main entrance of the Kṛṣṇa-Balarāma Mandir, an Indian gentleman hurriedly approached with his hands extended forward and downward, obviously intending to touch Śrīla Prabhupāda's lotus feet. We disciples were forbidden to do that, for had it been allowed, Śrīla Prabhupāda would have been imposed upon constantly. So I was surprised when Śrīla Prabhupāda stopped briefly to let the man fulfil his desire. It seemed to me that the man also wanted to say something to Śrīla Prabhupāda, who nonetheless continued walking into the temple. I thought, "If that man could do it, then why can't I also just go up and touch Śrīla Prabhupāda's lotus feet?" But there was strong social sanction against doing so.

On 4 April, Śrīla Prabhupāda held a large initiation ceremony in the courtyard of the Kṛṣṇa-Balarāma Mandir, during which I was to receive brahminical initiation. Almost seventy devotees were sitting to receive either first or second initiation, and because of the additional spectators the quadrangle was full. It was the beginning of summer and the sun was burning. Seated upon a *vyāsāsana*, Śrīla Prabhupāda oversaw the proceedings, with Akṣayānanda Swami performing the fire sacrifice.

* This is corroborated, at least in gist, by the following recorded statement by Tamāla Kṛṣṇa Goswami to Śrīla Prabhupāda: "I remember one boy was living there for about three months, and you got very angry and told him that there were already enough monkeys in Rādhā-kuṇḍa—do not try to jump over like a monkey." (Conversation, 7 June 1976)

"On 4 April, Śrīla Pr-abhupāda held a large initiation ceremony
Prabhupāda is seated at the top of the steps, his face obscured
Vikāsa Swami) is in the bottom left corner of the photo, second

A close-up of the same event. First from the left is Raṇajita Dāsa
Kāliyāphaṇi Dāsa (bare-chested).

in the courtyard of the Kṛṣṇa-Balarāma Mandir." (p. 19) Śrīla
by shadow and a microphone stand. Ilāpati Dāsa (later, Bhakti
from left in the front row, head down and barely discernible.

(wearing black-rimmed glasses), next is Ilāpati Dāsa, and third is

I was struck by Akṣayānanda Swami's tolerance in sitting next to the hot fire under the scorching Indian sun.

The sacrifice was well underway—*svāhā! svāhā!*—when suddenly Śrīla Prabhupāda leaned forward and spoke into the microphone: "Stop." Everything stopped. Śrīla Prabhupāda pointed to the back of the courtyard to one young Western lady devotee, who was holding on her lap a child not more than two years old. Śrīla Prabhupāda said, "This child has his hand in his mouth; he is contaminating the whole sacrifice. Take him out, wash his hand, and teach him not to put his hand in his mouth. Continue." Then the chanting of *svāhā* and the offering of oblations continued.

In that ceremony, there had been over thirty Gāyatrī initiates, and Śrīla Prabhupāda decided to personally give the mantra to each, a few every day. It was nearly a week later when I was called to receive the mantra. That morning I waited along with others outside Śrīla Prabhupāda's room. One by one they went in, until only I remained. Then Puṣṭa Kṛṣṇa Swami, Śrīla Prabhupāda's secretary, came out and told me, "Śrīla Prabhupāda is not seeing any more today. Come again tomorrow." Seeing my disappointment, Mahārāja told me to wait until the next devotee came out, and then go in. He told me to remove the black earthen Rādhā-kuṇḍa beads from my neck, explaining that Śrīla Prabhupāda did not like his disciples to wear them.

Now that I was at last within seconds of being close to Śrīla Prabhupāda, my head began to whirl. My eagerness became mixed with apprehension that I would act foolishly. But then I took shelter of my false pride, thinking that surely I (The Great I) would conduct myself properly and impress Śrīla Prabhupāda by how special and qualified I was. But soon (although it seemed like a long time) this tumble of speculations came to an end, because it was time for me to enter.

I strode into Śrīla Prabhupāda's room, trying to muster up the deep humility that I knew I should have, while simultaneously attempting to suppress my nervousness and feel confident. I bowed down and called to mind who Śrīla Prabhupāda was—the representative of the Supreme Personality of Godhead who had been sent to save the whole world, a pure devotee great even among pure devotees. Now I was all alone with Śrīla Prabhupāda and I did not know what to expect. But I did expect it to be profound.

Śrīla Prabhupāda instructed me how to sit in the proper position and at the right distance. He had to tell me three or four times before I got it right. I was dull-witted and could not understand exactly what Śrīla Prabhupāda wanted me to do. Then he told me to raise my right arm. I was becoming increasingly nervous, and it seemed that Śrīla Prabhupāda was growing a little impatient with me. He then draped the sacred thread upon my body—but with a little difficulty, because I did not hold my arm at a convenient angle.

Next, Śrīla Prabhupāda gave me a sheet of paper with the Gāyatrī mantra written on it and told me to repeat after him, word by word. Although I proudly considered myself competent in Sanskrit pronunciation, Śrīla Prabhupāda corrected almost every word that I spoke, and some words twice or thrice. Apparently considering me a hopeless case, Śrīla Prabhupāda soon stopped trying to rectify my pronunciation and just let me continue mispronouncing. After reciting all seven mantras, Śrīla Prabhupāda grasped my right hand and demonstrated how to wrap the thread around the thumb and keep count by moving the thumb along the joints of the fingers. He told me to mentally chant the mantras three times a day—morning, noon, and evening.

Then Śrīla Prabhupāda asked, "Do you have any questions?"

(In expectation of receiving the Gāyatrī mantra, my friend and *saṅkīrtana* partner from London, Satyavāk Prabhu, and myself had several times expectantly discussed this mystical Gāyatrī mantra and its wonderful effects. We had heard that the *Hari-bhakti-vilāsa* expounds many details to be followed while reciting the Gāyatrī mantra: exactly what time it should be chanted—for instance, so many minutes before sunrise; according to the time of day, whether to stand or sit; which direction to face and point the thumb; and which position to hold the hand. So when Śrīla Prabhupāda unexpectedly asked if I had any questions, I wanted to inquire about all these points. Mixed with my curiosity was an element of wanting Śrīla Prabhupāda to know that I had some esoteric śāstric knowledge.)

I began by asking, "Śrīla Prabhupāda, when should we chant these mantras?" Since he had just told me to chant in the morning, noon, and evening, Śrīla Prabhupāda looked at me somewhat surprisedly and repeated, "Morning, noon, and evening." Nonetheless, thinking that perhaps he had not understood that I was seeking a specific rather than general answer, I persisted: "But is there any specific, exact time when we should chant?" Śrīla Prabhupāda looked at me as if I were stupid—which I certainly was—and sternly said, "Morning, noon, and evening." After that, I no longer desired to ask Śrīla Prabhupāda any further questions about the intricacies of chanting the Gāyatrī mantra. I simply said, "Yes, Śrīla Prabhupāda." Feeling very foolish, I offered obeisance and left the room, having spoiled the only opportunity that I ever had to directly speak something pleasing to Śrīla Prabhupāda.

After the Vṛndāvana festival, I returned to England.

A little more than a year later, in August 1977, I went back to India with Trivikrama Swami, intending to remain there permanently for preaching. Soon after arriving in Delhi, we were on a bus to Vṛndāvana to have a brief *darśana* of Śrīla Prabhupāda before returning for service at ISKCON Delhi. Unfortunately, I have very little memory of that *darśana*. I was still jet-lagged, bus-shaken, and very much "in the modes." I could not realize my great fortune in again seeing Śrīla Prabhupāda. I did not know that I would see him only once more.

That final *darśana* was in October 1977, just one month before Śrīla Prabhupāda passed away. After a month in Delhi, I had joined the BBT Library Party, which was winding down its activities in India. We were in Allahabad, when early one morning Yajña Prabhu, the group leader, suddenly said, "Let's go take *darśana* of Śrīla Prabhupāda." We drove all day and arrived in Vṛndāvana in the evening. I was surprised at how easily we were allowed into Śrīla Prabhupāda's room. It was quite full, and a subdued, sweet *kīrtana* was going on. Yet I was saddened to see Śrīla Prabhupāda's condition. I never expected him to look so weak and thin. Had it been anyone else, it would have been understood that the person was about to die. But despite his prolonged sickness, most of Śrīla Prabhupāda's disciples never imagined that he would actually leave us, that he would not always be personally present to lead us. We thought his sickness to be a *līlā*, and that he would soon recover to again guide us as before.

That evening, Śrīla Prabhupāda asked the devotees attending him to raise him up so that he could eat something. Before honoring *prasāda*, he recited the entire prayer beginning *śarīra avidyā-jāl* and then began to explain its purport, that the senses are very dangerous. Even though for years Śrīla Prabhupāda had been preaching all over the world, he was still expounding the most basic point: control of the senses. He spoke slowly and

in a whisper, but with spiritual potency. Years later, I came to know that this was the first time in weeks that Śrīla Prabhupāda had eaten anything.

The next morning, I left Vṛndāvana to distribute books in Bengal. We knew that book distribution was very dear to Śrīla Prabhupāda, and we wanted to please him.

I never physically saw Śrīla Prabhupāda again.

Only out of His immense compassion does the Personality of Godhead reveal Himself as the spiritual master. Therefore in the dealings of an *ācārya* there are no activities but those of transcendental loving service to the Lord. He is the Supreme Personality of Servitor Godhead. It is worthwhile to take shelter of such a steady devotee, who is called *āśraya-vigraha,* or the manifestation or form of the Lord of whom one must take shelter.

(Cc *Ādi* 1.46, purport)

Thoughts on Serving Śrīla Prabhupāda in Separation

I saw Śrīla Prabhupāda. I heard him speak. Perhaps only briefly, but those memories are sustaining my life. At the time, I did not realize how valuable Śrīla Prabhupāda's personal association was, nor could I guess how soon it would be gone and that we would simply be left to weep. It seems like such a long time ago.

I know that Śrīla Prabhupāda is still watching over us. As much as we turn to him, to that degree he reciprocates with us. He is personally present, not intangibly.

But I am a fool, unable to properly perceive how Śrīla Prabhupāda is still fully with us. I want to see and hear him again, and again, and again. I am feeling very pained in his physical absence. Prabhupāda, please save me again!

You came into our lives, uncalled for, by your causeless mercy. You gave us the gift of devotional service to purify us and bring us to Kṛṣṇa. But because I am a rascal, I am not making progress. Rather, I am sinking ever deeper into *māyā*. Without your loving smiles and stern glances, I do not know how I will endure.

Śrīla Prabhupāda, when will I get the fortune to place your holy lotus feet on my head? When will I get the opportunity to again hear your voice and see you walk, dance, and sing?

Śrīla Prabhupāda, please protect this sentimental fool and make me your servant.

Then and Now: My Past and Present Lives

Sometimes devotees ask about my life before meeting Śrīla Prabhupāda, but I do not like to tell them. There are so many conditioned souls wandering in the universe, and there is no value in hearing about one more. For those who really want to know my previous life history, here it is: I was a dog.

I am still a dog, but now I am Śrīla Prabhupāda's dog. His mercy is all that I am made of.

> A practical example of *varṇa-saṅkara* is the hippies. No caste, no creed—neither useful for the material world, neither useful for the spiritual.[1]

That was my life before Śrīla Prabhupāda saved me.

Some devotees have deduced from astrology or hypnotic regression that in their last life they were a *pūjārī*, yogi, devotee, or whatever. I congratulate them on their exalted background. Personally, I have no knowledge of my previous life. I only know that after many, many lives of suffering in ignorance, Śrīla Prabhupāda saved me. I was in *māyā*—maybe as a *brāhmaṇa* or a Brahmā or a worm in stool, but in *māyā* I certainly was. This is beyond doubt, as evidenced by my still remaining deep-rooted envy and strong attachment to the objects of the senses.

Now my thoughts often move in a different direction. Today I was meditating on how to convince a confused man with whom I spoke last night. My life plans are to write, preach, and engage myself and others in Kṛṣṇa's service. Who can deny Prabhupāda's mercy on this wretched soul?

So my dear brothers, enjoy your previous-life speculation. I don't want it. I don't need it. I worship the dust of Śrīla Prabhupāda's lotus feet as my only treasure, for it was Śrīla Prabhupāda who saved me from the degradation of being sometimes a Brahmā and sometimes a worm in stool.

Associating with Śrīla Prabhupāda Through His Books

So now the devotees who wanted to know of my association with Śrīla Prabhupāda may be satisfied. Quantitatively there was not much to relate, but qualitatively, it is inexpressible by words. Although it might seem that, being a late-comer to ISKCON, I was destined to be distant from Śrīla Prabhupāda, spiritually I feel close to him. I am still associating with Śrīla Prabhupāda. Particularly when reading his books, I strongly feel his presence, as if he is speaking to me personally—which he is.

> The instruction given in my books is supposed to be personal instruction. When we read the *Bhagavad-gītā As It Is*, it is understood that we are receiving personal instructions of Kṛṣṇa. No physical barrier is there in the case of spiritual affairs.[2]

As Śrīla Prabhupāda often stressed, associating with him through *vāṇī,* the instructions in his books, is actual and direct association. Devotees are rightly eager to hear pastimes of Śrīla Prabhupāda, but he himself was more concerned that we imbibe his instructions and the philosophy of Kṛṣṇa consciousness—which he incessantly strived to inculcate—rather than simply hear narrations of his activities. And actually, Śrīla Prabhupāda's actions centered around his dispensing of instruction. Both by precept and by practice, day and night he was instructing—delivering lectures, dictating scriptural commentaries, giving personal guidance, and so on. The essence of all his advice is in

his books, and thus he declared, "If you want to know me, read my books."

As is the case with so many devotees, whatever has happened to me in Kṛṣṇa consciousness began with reading one of Śrīla Prabhupāda's books. Looking back at what the *Kṛṣṇa* book did for me, I can very confidently declare that Śrīla Prabhupāda's books are not really books at all, at least not in the ordinary sense. They are not simply pieces of paper with ink on them. Śrīla Prabhupāda's books are mercy incarnations of Kṛṣṇa in literary form, presenting Himself through His chosen representative. Kṛṣṇa is personally present in every letter, along with His pure devotee Śrīla Prabhupāda. It must be so. Otherwise, how could those words alter and uplift lives as they do?

Other devotees may be claimed as more eloquent or scholarly than Śrīla Prabhupāda. But no one's books can penetrate the heart—and of so many people—as do Śrīla Prabhupāda's. That is why, although apparently quite simple, Śrīla Prabhupāda's books have unparalleled potency. Nor are they mere primers, to be read before graduating to "higher things." They are supremely authoritative because they are Kṛṣṇa. As Śrīla Prabhupāda himself indicated, within his books he has presented everything needed to become fully Kṛṣṇa conscious.[3] "Everything" means *everything*. Like the bottomless wells found at several holy places in India, Śrīla Prabhupāda's books may seem ordinary but actually have no end.

Of course, Śrīla Prabhupāda's books are masterpieces of erudition that are recognized by scholars throughout the world. But they go far beyond ordinary academics. In every line, every word, Śrīla Prabhupāda urges us to surrender to Kṛṣṇa. Moreover, with every reading we get fresh inspiration of the pressing need to share this knowledge with others.

I bow down to Śrīla Prabhupāda's books and worship them. I worship Śrīla Prabhupāda, who came to me in the form of his books and saved me. All glories to Śrīla Prabhupāda, who expands himself as his books, which go to every nook and cranny of the world, searching out lost followers like guided missiles. They pierce through thick crusts of false ego and reach the soul, who then awakens from his long slumber and wonders, "O Kṛṣṇa, how have I forgotten you?"

Associating with Śrīla Prabhupāda Through Service

I felt very intensely Śrīla Prabhupāda's presence in the early days of our preaching mission in Bangladesh. There were but few devotees and we were spread thin. I had to spend weeks and months without strong association. It was underground work, with constant difficulties. I was forced to call to Śrīla Prabhupāda for help, and his mercy was the vital factor that kept me going.

Once I was traveling alone in Bangladesh and, for want of devotee association, feeling forlorn and estranged from everything around me. Ahead was a full day's journey to the capital, Dhaka, on bumpy roads in a hot, noisy, crowded bus. I had just recovered from a severe fever and was still groggy and weak. People were talking loudly and smoking, and goats and chickens inside the bus added extra noise and smells. Suddenly I thought, "Why am I doing this?" For a short time I was bewildered—until I remembered that I was doing it for Śrīla Prabhupāda. Then all the hardship seemed insignificant. Rather, it seemed a great privilege to have an opportunity to accept some trouble in service to Śrīla Prabhupāda.

It was definitely all worth it. Prabhupāda went through so many difficulties to save us, so we should be grateful for the privilege to endure some minor difficulties for the sake of pleasing him.

Remembering Śrīla Prabhupāda

Remembering Śrīla Prabhupāda is not just a sentiment or fancy to be indulged in from time to time. Remembering Śrīla Prabhupāda is the very essence of our existence.

Not only when reading, but throughout the day, every day, remembrance of Śrīla Prabhupāda continues as we serve his mission. If we are not still associating with Śrīla Prabhupāda, then what are we living for and what are we preaching about? My relationship with Śrīla Prabhupāda is not limited to memories of a few incidents that terminated in 1977. That relationship is not limited by time and space. It is real now and will be forever. If that were not true, then all of us might as well die now, for what would be the meaning to life without Śrīla Prabhupāda and Kṛṣṇa?

Remembrance of Śrīla Prabhupāda is not limited to anecdotes from the past. Our whole life, from now unto eternity, should be surcharged with meditation on Śrīla Prabhupāda and his mission. Kṛṣṇa says, "Always think of Me," and we cannot think of Him without thinking of Śrīla Prabhupāda. It is Śrīla Prabhupāda who gave us Kṛṣṇa, so we are inextricably linked with him eternally. We do not want anything, not even Kṛṣṇa consciousness, without Śrīla Prabhupāda. For us in ISKCON, there is no meaning to Kṛṣṇa consciousness without Śrīla Prabhupāda. We do not want anything outside of that.

It is up to us to choose to either remember or forget Śrīla Prabhupāda, or to confabulate him as something that he is not.

Relationship with Śrīla Prabhupāda

I and many others practically perceive how the relationship with the spiritual master is not based on physical presence. I joined ISKCON as a young kid in 1975, when it was already a large worldwide organization. There was no question of just walking up to Śrīla Prabhupāda and talking to him, nor even of getting an appointment to see him. We could attend lectures and *darśanas* but felt (and I certainly was) too insignificant to ask him a question, even in the public forum. We could not even write to him, for we were told not to disturb him with letters. We were instructed simply to serve his mission and that that would be our relationship with him. So we did, and I did not feel anything lacking in my connection to Śrīla Prabhupāda. I worked for him and prayed to him, fully believing in his transcendental ability to accept and respond to my offerings. It might appear that we never even really met, but we did. Otherwise, how could I offer my self and all my actions to Śrīla Prabhupāda, and how could he accept those offerings? On the material platform we hardly met, but we certainly did meet on the spiritual platform.

Even though I saw very little of Śrīla Prabhupāda, he effected a total change in every aspect of my life. Not only was my whole attitude and understanding of life transformed, but even my dress, food, mannerisms, and use of language. How was all of this possible with so little personal contact? The answer is that I did, and still do, have contact with him. If I did not, then what is the meaning of the guru-disciple relationship? Service to the spiritual master is never impersonal. It is always personal. The spiritual master is a person, the disciple is a person, and the bond between them is personal. Spiritual relationships are not limited by material time and space.

Some disciples of Śrīla Prabhupāda never even saw him at all, but their intimate relationship with him continues to sustain their life in Kṛṣṇa consciousness. Materialists cannot understand this. They would call it imagination. But it is not. Our relationship with Śrīla Prabhupāda is deep and real, whereas those of the material world are false and transitory, certain to dissolve in course of time. But even when Śrīla Prabhupāda was present on this planet, relationships with him did not depend on physical proximity. Śrīla Prabhupāda's departure from this planet did not terminate the thousands of loving relationships he had established with disciples and others. That which is spiritual is ever increasing.

I have felt how my relationship with Śrīla Prabhupāda developed more and more after his departure. Surely this is true of all his disciples, especially those who faithfully continue to follow his instructions. And there are many others who established their relationship with Śrīla Prabhupāda after his physical departure from this world—proof indeed that a Vaiṣṇava lives in sound.

In material relationships, generally after a person dies he gradually fades from others' memory, and bereaved persons learn to live without a departed relative. But we are learning to live *with* Śrīla Prabhupāda. Our closeness to him simply increases day by day.

How close do we want to be to Śrīla Prabhupāda? It's up to us. He is ready to fully accept us. But are we ready to fully accept him?

Who Knows Śrīla Prabhupāda Best?

Do those devotees who lived intimately with Śrīla Prabhupāda in the early days, or were his secretaries and traveling companions, or were directly trained by him know Śrīla Prabhupāda best?

In some ways the answer must be yes. But in a more spiritually realistic sense, they who know him best are those who have kept themselves open to his mercy by making his instructions their life.

> Personal service to the spiritual master means to follow his instructions. My request is the same for everyone: that they follow strictly the regulative principles and chant at least sixteen rounds daily. And as much time as they are able should be devoted for preaching according to our books.[4]

By their faithfulness, disciples who have continued to serve Śrīla Prabhupāda through the days, weeks, months, and years have proved their commitment to his mission and their realization of his instructions. That is true not only of his direct disciples but of all his followers in disciplic succession. Śrīla Prabhupāda himself had limited personal association with Śrīla Bhaktisiddhānta Sarasvatī Ṭhākura, but his activities showed that he knew the heart of his guru-mahārāja.

On Representing Śrīla Prabhupāda

Nowadays I am getting many letters, mostly from people whom I have met on preaching travels or who have read my books. Many ask for advice, and I reply, advising as Śrīla Prabhupāda advised us. Respondents often express tremendous gratefulness. People become so enlivened to get (what seems to me to be straightforward) advice such as, "Try to chant Hare Kṛṣṇa attentively and read Śrīla Prabhupāda's books every day." So much affection is being showered on me through the mail. I hardly feel capable to reciprocate it.

Śrīla Prabhupāda! You said, "Just do as I am doing," and I am trying to do that. But whereas you have unlimited goodwill and compassion, I am limited by lust, greed, anger, desire for name and fame, and so many other wicked desires. Your knowledge, realization, and genuine concern for others are unbounded. Mine hardly exists.

Śrīla Prabhupāda! Please quickly rescue me from my deficiencies. I want to be your servant, but am hardly fit to be so. If I could reflect even a particle of your exalted qualities and convey them to others, I might then begin to serve you properly. May I love others at least a fraction as much as you love them.

This morning I was looking at a photo of Śrīla Prabhupāda *(see opposite)* sitting erect on the *vyāsāsana,* appearing most aristocratic and determined, playing a gong and wearing a huge beautiful flower garland; the *vyāsāsana* is also profusely decorated with flowers. To pick flowers and string them into an elaborate garland takes time, care, and feeling.

> You are giving me so many garlands. Why are you giving me? Because you love me. Otherwise there was no necessity. Because you have got some love, therefore you are worshiping your spiritual master.[5]

Sometimes devotees also offer me a similarly decorated seat and a gorgeous garland, so while looking at that photo I thought, "All the nice garlands should be offered to Kṛṣṇa and Śrīla Prabhupāda, but now they are offering them to me also." I am not even a millionth part able to reciprocate as Śrīla Prabhupāda did. His compassion, his caring, and his feeling are all unlimited. I am simply trying to follow in his footsteps, praying that his qualities may be reflected in me, at least in traces. I will neither refuse the garlands nor pretend to be as good as Śrīla Prabhupāda. I will accept the love and affection of the devotees, offer it to Śrīla Prabhupāda, and reciprocate with the devotees as best I can by instructing them as Śrīla Prabhupāda instructed us.

Made of His Mercy

That as an ISKCON sannyasi and direct disciple of Śrīla Prabhupāda I am honored and respected—especially by devotees who never personally saw Śrīla Prabhupāda—is another testimony to Śrīla Prabhupāda's greatness. Because of the relationship that Śrīla Prabhupāda's disciples have with him, the next generation of devotees in ISKCON accord great respect to them. Before meeting Śrīla Prabhupāda, we were all ordinary people, destined for lower species of life. Śrīla Prabhupāda saved us. We must never forget that we are all made of his mercy. To the extent that we remember this and go on boldly and enthusiastically propagating his mission, the Kṛṣṇa consciousness movement will be successful. Conversely, to the degree that we forget through whom the potency to spread Kṛṣṇa consciousness is coming, that much we will simply have to suffer due to not properly recognizing the source of our blessings.

I am some kind of leader in this Hare Krishna movement. As a sannyasi, initiating guru, and writer of strongly worded books, I have taken a stand against *māyā*. Sannyasis are meant to generate faith in devotional service by their exemplary behavior. If I were to fall from such a standard, it would be bad not only for me but also for others, especially my disciples. I cannot claim to have conquered *māyā*, as did one of our foolish godbrothers. He appeared to have attained mighty heights, but was kicked by *māyā* into nasty depths. How was it possible? Because he forgot his position as servant of Śrīla Prabhupāda. He was but one of several devotees in our society who attained extraordinary opulence and power in devotional service, performed exceptional activities, and then fell down. This caused chaos throughout our movement. It was especially disastrous for their disciples, few of whom ever really recovered from the shock. My activities are minuscule compared to what some of these great *saṅkīrtana* generals accomplished.

Śrīla Prabhupāda, your mercy is all that I am made of. I have taken this great risk of *sannyāsa* only to serve your lotus feet. Yet I am not very competent to serve you. So many godbrothers and disciples of godbrothers are doing far more than I to please you. Śrīla Prabhupāda, this is not a very exalted prayer, but one that I need to make: "Please don't let me fall down." Even you were praying like that, you told us. The difference is that you had no need to, although out of humility you may have felt that you did. For me, it is a real prayer that I cannot put enough energy into.

Prabhupāda Knows Everything

Sometimes devotees see me, a sannyasi, and ask, "How have you become so spiritually advanced?" Of course, I know more about my true position than they do. Simply to officially accept *sannyāsa* is no cure for the nonsense mind. But I never doubted anything Prabhupāda wrote or said. I know that everything given by Śrīla Prabhupāda is right. Prabhupāda knows Kṛṣṇa and therefore knows everything. If anyone thinks that Śrīla Prabhupāda ever made any fundamental mistake, then that person has committed the gravest mistake.

Over the years, occasionally doubts have momentarily presented themselves while I read Prabhupāda's books. But to kill such demonic doubts, I immediately call on Prabhupāda's logic: "You have to believe someone." So then I ask myself, "Do you believe Prabhupāda and the *ācāryas*, or the demons who are envious of God?" And that is the end of the doubt: "Śrīla Prabhupāda is correct."

Even if his statements appear to be apparently contradictory or against all contemporary so-called scientific logic and reason—no problem. Quoting from *śāstra*, Śrīla Prabhupāda has said:

"The moon is farther away than the sun."[6] "It is a heavenly planet,"[7] with "rivers of nectar."[8]

"Pigeons can be trained to carry one into outer space."[9]

"Giant eagles fly from one planet to another, and while flying they lay eggs."[10]

If Prabhupāda says so, it must be correct. Even if it seems impossible or contradictory, there must be a transcendental explanation. If it seems scientifically incorrect, then the scientists must be wrong. I do not have to research everything; others may research later. Even if I do research a subtle or technical point, it is only for clarification, for I know that Śrīla Prabhupāda can never be wrong. Even if, due to rascaldom or weakness, I do not always fully implement Prabhupāda's instructions, at least I never doubt them. Caitanya Mahāprabhu also declared His firm belief in the words of His spiritual master, even against the popular opinion prevalent at that time, and indicated that this is the sure way to make spiritual advancement.[11] This attitude might be considered small-minded or fanatical, but it has not rendered me unintelligent. I am prepared to argue with anyone, utilizing logic, reason, and scriptural knowledge to substantiate any point made by Śrīla Prabhupāda. It is the solace of our life to associate with devotees of the same conviction.

Prabhupāda Days

By their culture, Indian people are trained to accept, respect, and even love their guru. Of course, there is no such tradition in the West. Śrīla Prabhupāda evoked immense affection and dedication from his disciples, who were drawn to him by his purity, compassion, and other tremendous spiritual qualities. East and West, outsiders were astonished by the guru-*bhakti* of Śrīla Prabhupāda's followers. That effusive love startled airport-goers as it burst out in an unrestrained overflow of weeping, leaping, thundering drums and *karatālas*, flower-showers, and roaring of "*Jaya* Prabhupāda! *Jaya* Prabhupāda!" The devotees were so anxious to see their beloved Prabhupāda that they were hardly aware that others existed, let alone be concerned about what others thought. That weeping was real. Nor did the devotees show their love only at exuberant airport arrivals, but also day after day in the streets, parking lots, and malls—ardently passing out Prabhupāda's books.

Śrīla Prabhupāda brought waves of spiritual ecstasy. When he was personally present, the movement had a very special atmosphere. Walking off the street into a temple was like directly entering the spiritual world. Devotees were so innocent, almost naive it may seem, but they had firm faith in Śrīla Prabhupāda and Kṛṣṇa, and their faces shone. Everything was "nectar," "ecstasy," "bliss"—really. Sure, there were also falldowns, jockeying for top positions, and so on, but still, the atmosphere was joyful and confident—"simply wonderful." "Everything's OK because Śrīla Prabhupāda is here."

As Satsvarūpa Mahārāja reminisced:

> What bliss and "luxury" to count on seeing Prabhupāda at least a few times a year! We called that "serving in separation." Nowadays there is no such hope of catching up with Prabhupāda in Atlanta, or at least seeing him once a year in India. We did not know how much we had until we lost it. What we have now is also very deep and wonderful, and can be filled with Prabhupāda consciousness.

> The devotees at the Māyāpur festival would hang on Prabhupāda's every word and discuss them and desire to carry them out. There were inevitable clashes of false ego and power politics among the leaders who sought to be "prominent," although Prabhupāda said that was material. But with an astounding ability to manage us all, Prabhupāda extracted service from each person, and kept us together as a more or less harmonious camp. Everything was for Kṛṣṇa and for spreading Kṛṣṇa consciousness to the world. For our vision we looked to Śrīla Prabhupāda. We all acknowledged that we could not see, but we had full faith that he could see. He was compassionate for the suffering of the world; he could defeat the nonsense. No one could defeat him. We walked beside him on the morning walks like little children, and yet like soldiers ready to fight the enemy on his word.[12]

Śrīla Prabhupāda's Fighting Spirit

Śrīla Prabhupāda was a fighter. Throughout his life he struggled against the indifference of his wife and children. Just to board the Jaladuta, he had to overcome more indifference, plus disbelief and governmental red tape. He landed in America a lone fighter, armed with the sword of knowledge. After taking stock of the battle ahead, he proceeded to hack away at the worldliness that epitomized America.

He was against modern "slaughterhouse" education and the grossly materialistic "build and break" society. Yet although much of what he said appealed to the nonconformist, anti-establishment hippie outlook, Śrīla Prabhupāda also did not compromise with the noncommittal, whimsical attitude typical of hippies. He saw through their motivated cries for peace, their pleas to end the Vietnam war so that they could continue peacefully enjoying sense gratification. He was against free sex, contraception, abortion, feminism, homosexuality, and even heterosexuality not meant for producing Kṛṣṇa conscious children. Laziness, uncleanness, and vague so-called "spirituality" were all kicked out by Śrīla Prabhupāda.

Śrīla Prabhupāda decried cheating swamis and bogus incarnations of God. He decried karma, *jñāna,* yoga, demigod worship, *smārta*-ism, Māyāvāda, *sahajiyā*-ism, mixed devotion, and the bodily concept of life. He was against rising later than four o'clock in the morning, and indeed anything less than pure devotional service to Kṛṣṇa.

He berated the United Nations when no one else dreamed to do so. He exposed those who claimed to be gentlemen simply by wearing a suit and tie. He spoke against meat-eating, communism, complacency, the mechanized consumer society, modern city life, cruelty to trees, and the false theory of overpopulation.

Śrīla Prabhupāda dispelled the illusion that anyone can be happy by any means except pure devotional service to Kṛṣṇa. He was for Kṛṣṇa only, and against anything conceived without relation to Kṛṣṇa.

Śrīla Prabhupāda's Risks and Difficulties

When we say that a preacher takes risks, it does not mean only physical risks. He also risks his reputation and his own spiritual standing. For instance, to award *dīkṣā,* especially to less-qualified candidates, is a risk, for the falldown of a disciple may be construed as a blot on the guru. Śrīla Prabhupāda took tremendous risks. He initiated not a few, but several thousand, disciples from undisciplined, uncultured backgrounds. He gave *sannyāsa* to unlikely candidates—young men fresh from irresponsible, hedonistic hippie life, fledgling devotees who knew little Sanskrit beyond the few *ślokas* they could mispronounce. Śrīla Prabhupāda established the worship of Śrī Śrī Rādhā-Kṛṣṇa by *mlecchas,* although he could not be sure how the Deities would be treated in the future.

Even though many failed to live up to Śrīla Prabhupāda's hopes, there is no question of blaming Śrīla Prabhupāda, for he did it all without the slightest motive for personal gain or aggrandizement. He declared that his "misdeed" was to accept "nonsense disciples."[13] He also wrote: "The spiritual master accepts the sinful activities of his disciples from the first initiation. I may give initiation very easily, but what can I do? I am prepared to go to hell for the service of Lord Caitanya."[14] We should not take lightly the risks Śrīla Prabhupāda accepted for our sake, and should remain ever grateful to him for extending such extraordinary mercy to us, especially considering that no other Gauḍīya Vaiṣṇava among Śrīla Prabhupāda's contemporaries was even thinking about how to benefit the sinful and fallen persons of the Western world. In reciprocation, as Śrīla Prabhupāda gave himself to us, we also should give ourselves to him and to others, by endeavoring to fulfil his expectations.

Śrīla Prabhupāda's *līlā* on this planet was not all joy and victory. Much of it makes us wince, as we recall what Prabhupāda went through to bring Kṛṣṇa to us. He struggled alone in the streets of Delhi and New York, sometimes without proper clothing or food. After starting his movement, Śrīla Prabhupāda occasionally had to deal with unsubmissive, disrespectful, or even rebellious disciples. A few disciples even tried to dominate Prabhupāda, or argued with or openly defied him. We do not like to hear of or mention these things, but seen in retrospect, they teach us how an ideal *ācārya* responds to highly distasteful behavior. We also gain insight into a particular risk that a preacher and

spiritual master takes—that disciples may behave obnoxiously toward their guru. We see how Prabhupāda was not afraid to "get his hands dirty," confront any obstacle, or take any risk in his ongoing challenge against *māyā*.

All glories to you, our dearly beloved Śrīla Prabhupāda! You saved us by force, despite our contrary natures. Following in your footsteps, your true followers cannot neglect the unpleasant realities that must be faced to further your mission.

Śrīla Prabhupāda's Influence

Just see the influence of Śrīla Prabhupāda! Lying on his bed in Vṛndāvana at the final stage of his life, he was hardly able to move, eat, or speak. Yet without even doing anything or going anywhere, he was inspiring his disciples around the world to distribute his books in unprecedented numbers. His going to London in that condition was another incredible pastime that clearly sets Śrīla Prabhupāda apart from the rest. There his disciples danced with full energy before their almost completely immobile spiritual master. And when Śrīla Prabhupāda moved his finger slightly, to indicate that they should dance even more enthusiastically, the devotees went wild and almost jumped through the ceiling. Śrīla Prabhupāda's influence came not from mind control, bribery, or force but was born of deep and powerful love.

Had Prabhupāda Stayed Just a Little Longer

During Śrīla Prabhupāda's manifest presence, the Kṛṣṇa consciousness movement grew tremendously. It resembled an unstoppable steamroller crushing Kali-yuga, an enormous expanding power that we expected would very soon engulf the world. While Śrīla Prabhupāda was with us, we expected the most amazing things to happen.

Śrīla Prabhupāda was a conqueror for Kṛṣṇa. He always thought big: "Double book distribution each year"; "Drive agnosticism out of the world"; "Make America Kṛṣṇa conscious first, then the rest of the world will follow"; "Prevent nuclear war by distributing books in Russia"; "Unite India, Pakistan, Bangladesh, Burma, and Sri Lanka on the basis of Kṛṣṇa consciousness"; "Millions will join our farms."

Had Śrīla Prabhupāda stayed with us, would he not have continued to push on irresistibly? Would he not have had the entire world talking of Kṛṣṇa? Would he not have shaken the scientific and pseudo-intellectual communities by his repeated attacks on their foolish theories? Would he not have turned the world into a battlefield of Kṛṣṇa consciousness versus *māyā*, himself out on the front lines as the commander of the troops? Would he not have sustained the spiritual life of his disciples, established *daiva-varṇāśrama-dharma* farm communities, and forstalled the terrible strife that ensued in his absence?

In India, Śrīla Prabhupāda had a special mission. Would he not have organized everything there on a mass scale, with hundreds and thousands of initiated disciples? Would he not have had followers from the highest echelons of society, including top businessmen and politicians, followers from the intellectuals and middle classes, and also from the simple village folk and urban working class? Would he not have captured the attention of the entire country and become established as the overwhelmingly prominent sadhu of the modern age? Would he not have reduced the bogus incarnations (over three hundred at latest count) and cheating swamis to their proper status as mere glowworms? Would he not have saved Bhārata from her confused descent into utter materialism? Would he not have won the respect and love of even the Muslim community? Would he not have made Indians proud to be Kṛṣṇa conscious? Would he not have driven out gross sinful activities, revived the original Vedic culture, and established India as the world's first spiritual superpower?

Had Śrīla Prabhupāda stayed, he certainly would have done far more than all of our bumbling efforts combined. Why then did he leave so early? The answer is not easy to fathom. Maybe he wanted us to become responsible, to do the father's work without forever remaining dependent children. Quite likely, he felt the urgent need to establish Kṛṣṇa consciousness in another part of this universe or in another universe. As Śrīla Prabhupāda said of his own guru-mahārāja:

> Bhaktisiddhānta Sarasvatī Ṭhākura, our spiritual master, came in this world to execute the mission of Caitanya Mahāprabhu. So he executed it, and when it was required, he left this place and went to another place to do the same business.[15]

Ultimately, only Kṛṣṇa and Śrīla Prabhupāda know why he left us when he did. Whatever the reason may be, Śrīla Prabhupāda has now gone away. He gave us a taste for Kṛṣṇa consciousness, showed us what to do, instructed us how to eternally associate with the spiritual master through service, and then moved on. One day all of us will have to fly our own plane.

On Śrīla Prabhupāda's Spiritual Revolution

Every devotee has his own relationship with and vision of Śrīla Prabhupāda. Some conceive him as their father, others as their best friend, and yet others approach him in great awe and reverence as their worshipful master. Many devotees related to Prabhupāda as a transcendental general, the leader of the troops. Personally, I like to meditate on Śrīla Prabhupāda as a revolutionary.

Like many of my generation, from an early age I knew there was something intrinsically wrong about the modern world. I felt that this material civilization and all it represents is totally bogus and nasty and needs to be turned upside down (i.e., putting it the right way up)—a complete revamping from top to bottom. All the so-called great thinkers who had tried to solve the world's problems had failed. Śrīla Prabhupāda was the first true revolutionary. Trashing all mundane ideas, he went to the root of all problems. He advocated total change, a change of consciousness: "Don't try to be an exploiter. Recognize your position as servant, not master." Śrīla Prabhupāda caught our mood—not with gimmicks, but from the platform of realization. He could not tolerate seeing all humanity wasting their lives, preparing to go to hell instead of to Kṛṣṇa. He blasted everything: the United Nations, slaughterhouse schools, rock'n'roll, automobile whoosh-whoosh. According to Prabhupāda, even Ravi Shankar's sitar ragas were sense gratification.

For Kṛṣṇa's sake, Śrīla Prabhupāda was ready to take on a world full of demons. As Kṛṣṇa's humble servant, he was always confident of Kṛṣṇa's support. He fearlessly targeted the world's leaders as the main culprits, the "thought criminals" who are misdirecting the world. But Śrīla Prabhupāda was nothing like the loud-mouthed rebels who want to demolish the status quo simply to establish another variety of illusion. Śrīla Prabhupāda brought the real revolution. Revolution means "complete turnaround." Śrīla Prabhupāda brought us from the mundane to Kṛṣṇa. Not only did he point out the failings of modern society, but he gave us substantive reality—Kṛṣṇa, the

Supreme Personality of Godhead—as the actual alternative. Now that Śrīla Prabhupāda has shown us the actual problem, forgetfulness of Kṛṣṇa, we can understand that all so-called great thinkers are actually blind men groping about with no idea of what is really going on.

Yet Śrīla Prabhupāda was not merely an armchair critic. He was not content simply to criticize, but wanted to make a practical and valuable contribution to human society. Of course, a reformer must also be a critic, for how can he effect improvement without first pinpointing the problems? Because only Śrīla Prabhupāda could perceive the actual problems, only he could be a genuine reformer. He saw poverty, injustice, crime, and the rest as manifestations of the fundamental anomaly: enviousness of Kṛṣṇa. "Who is wronged, and who is the wrongdoer? Who is a criminal, and who is a victim? All are criminals—all need reforming," he taught us. Therefore Śrīla Prabhupāda did not waste his time making useless niceties such as hospitals to make people fit for sense gratification, or schools for training in sense gratification. He gave the blueprint for an alternative society with Kṛṣṇa at the center. He started farm communities for simple living and high thinking, depending on the land, the cows, and Kṛṣṇa.

Śrīla Prabhupāda gave a lifestyle that rejected and transcended materialistic values. No hard work for sense gratification. No divorce. No democracy. No false equality. No anything without Kṛṣṇa. He wanted society organized into *varṇas* and *āśramas,* with ideal, peaceful *brāhmaṇas* giving direction to powerful pious kings. He wanted women to be chaste, shy, and submissive to their husbands—no feminism, just happy women. He wanted cow protection. He wanted all of this in the world today.

Śrīla Prabhupāda's idea was clear, and we all knew it: "Kṛṣṇa consciousness will lead the world." Although our numbers

were tiny and we may have seemed like just another frivolous cult, we were surcharged with Prabhupāda's confidence and experienced the power of Kṛṣṇa in ISKCON. We were dynamic and buoyant—at least up till 1977. We naively believed that nothing could go wrong, that if we just kept on chanting Hare Kṛṣṇa, passing out the books, and following the GBC, then Kṛṣṇa consciousness would take over the world. As Śrīla Prabhupāda said, "History will mark this period, how Kṛṣṇa consciousness changed the world."[16]

But Śrīla Prabhupāda also warned that disunity of his movement would be detrimental to its missionary purpose.[17] Unfortunately, much of what happened during the years just after Prabhupāda's departure is an unhappy testimony to those prophetic words. Nowadays, it seems that our movement has lost the vision for making this planet, and ultimately the whole universe, Kṛṣṇa conscious. Many devotees who joined ISKCON after Śrīla Prabhupāda's disappearance are apparently unaware of his revolutionary mood.

No longer clearly united in purpose, members of ISKCON nevertheless remain together, remembering Śrīla Prabhupāda's ominous warning: "Your love for me will be tested how after my departure you maintain this institution."[18] Probably we took that statement too lightly. Maybe we were overconfident about how much we loved Śrīla Prabhupāda, or took it for granted that unity and purity would easily be maintained. We probably did not sufficiently appreciate the tremendous power of Śrīla Prabhupāda's personal presence toward offsetting the divisive influence of Kali-yuga.

Whatever may have caused the ensuing misfortune, the challenge still stands before us: "Your love for me will be tested how after my departure you maintain this institution." The success of our mission depends upon it.

Therefore we should meditate on how to really cooperate to please Śrīla Prabhupāda—not like the United Nations, who join together for meetings but remain forever divided. Let us pray to Śrīla Prabhupāda for the intelligence to serve him properly. All of us have dedicated our life to the same mission. We believe the same thing, read the same books, and (should) preach the same philosophy. While differences of approach will always be there, our *siddhānta* is one. Learning to really work together, not just cosmetically, is the key to and measure of our success. Our bond is our love for Śrīla Prabhupāda. We may disagree with each other, sometimes even vigorously, but one point we all agree on is that we should please Śrīla Prabhupāda. Coming together on the platform of glorifying Śrīla Prabhupāda and Kṛṣṇa is our only hope.

The unifying principle in our movement of strong-minded persons is submission to and faith in the orders of Śrīla Prabhupāda. Cooperation means becoming humble and subduing our egos. It is difficult, but purifying. We must cooperate, because that is one of Śrīla Prabhupāda's most important instructions. Without cooperating, we will be lost, both individually and collectively. That we have developed strong minds is a sign of Śrīla Prabhupāda's success, but a further sign of his success is our continuing to respectfully live, work, and cooperate together despite our personal and philosophical differences, even though Śrīla Prabhupāda is not physically present to pacify us. If the spirit of cooperating to please Śrīla Prabhupāda is strong, even strong differences can be tolerated.

We must look to the future. Lamenting over the past will not help. Personally, I am convinced that Śrīla Prabhupāda's desire for a Kṛṣṇa conscious world civilization will manifest. Śrīla Prabhupāda wanted it, and Kṛṣṇa will fulfil his desire.

The Kṛṣṇa consciousness movement is carrying the potency of Kṛṣṇa. Nothing is impossible for Kṛṣṇa and His pure devotees.

Our movement still bears the energy of the Supreme Lord. We have the best philosophy, the best process, the best guru, and the blessings of the most merciful avatar, Śrī Caitanya Mahāprabhu. With His benediction we can blaze forward and save the world.

> Everywhere there is a great chance to give this Kṛṣṇa consciousness movement a great push, and if we do everything very carefully there is no reason why we cannot save the world.[19]

Those who undertake the missionary work in a selfless mood will be successful. Śrīla Prabhupāda has given us practical solutions to the myriad problems that bedevil the world. We simply have to become instruments in his hands and he will reveal how everything should be done. Either we will do it, or others will—now or in the future—but happen it will. As Śrīla Prabhupāda said, it is up to us to take the credit or not.

This is the most exciting period in the world's history. We are most fortunate to have the rare opportunity to take part in Lord Caitanya's and Śrīla Prabhupāda's spiritual revolution. Caitanya Mahāprabhu wanted that there be chanting in every town and village of the world. True, there is still a long way to go. But if we simply stick faithfully and intelligently to Śrīla Prabhupāda's instructions, we will see the course of world history undergoing tremendous changes that few people can now imagine.

The implementation of the cultural revolution to save the world is presently in the hands of Śrīla Prabhupāda's followers. One symptom of a devotee who has taken Śrīla Prabhupāda's mission seriously is a sense of purpose and urgency. He is aware of the multiple tasks that must be undertaken for spreading Kṛṣṇa consciousness and diligently applies himself in a productive, focused manner to help expand this movement. He is not lazy.

Prabhupāda Consciousness

It is not very difficult to be Prabhupāda conscious and to have his association. There is no need to make any special arrangement or strain our brains about it. We just have to throw ourselves into the fire of preaching. This does not mean merely giving a casual lecture here and there, but immersing ourselves day and night in thoughts of how to push on Prabhupāda's mission, within our given capacity. We have to absorb ourselves in preaching activities. When we speak to someone about Kṛṣṇa or try to induce him to take a book, we should pray, "Please, Śrīla Prabhupāda, help me convince these people." When asked questions or challenged, we should try to remember how Prabhupāda replied to such queries. When tempted by *māyā*, we should say, "No!" because we know it would be displeasing to Śrīla Prabhupāda and a hindrance to our full absorption in his service. When we face the inevitable difficulties in preaching, we should remember how Prabhupāda tolerated all inconveniences, patiently overcame all obstacles, and persevered undisturbed, pushing forward his movement.

Another aspect of being Prabhupāda conscious is to offer all our successes back to him. We are made of his mercy and have no separate abilities of our own. All guidance, inspiration, and blessings come from him.

Śrīla Prabhupāda's Movement

Śrīla Prabhupāda was sent by Lord Caitanya to fulfil His mission of spreading Kṛṣṇa consciousness all over the world.

There is no doubt that this mission will become prominent and lead the world, for it is the desire of Lord Caitanya and Śrīla Prabhupāda. This movement is destined to be fabulously successful, and it will happen when those who purport to be followers of Śrīla Prabhupāda clearly understand that ISKCON was, is, and always will be Prabhupāda's mission. Everything belongs to Śrīla Prabhupāda; nothing is ours. We are absolutely and always his servants.

We do not have dozens of movements with dozens of leaders, but one movement with a single leader. Within this mission there may be many departments with their respective leaders, but the ultimate leader is one. Our duty is to conjointly serve Prabhupāda's mission. Let us try to be great servants of our great master and serve his servants also. That is Vaiṣṇava philosophy. Although most devotees within ISKCON are guided by various disciples of Śrīla Prabhupāda, there should not be much difference between those disciples or between subsequent discipular descendants, for we are all members of Śrīla Prabhupāda's family.

ISKCON is nondifferent from Śrīla Prabhupāda—"my body," he said. Someone may purport to love Prabhupāda yet dislike ISKCON, but that is like declaring love for Kṛṣṇa but repugnance for His cows. Whatever ISKCON is, was, or should be, it is inseparable from Śrīla Prabhupāda. If we really love Śrīla Prabhupāda, we can never reject ISKCON. Whatever difficulties or failings may exist, we must remain in this movement and try to overcome the problems that inevitably will arise by the very nature of this condemned world. Instead of demanding utopia, we must learn to live in this world and do something practical to make it better, by working to help make Śrīla Prabhupāda's mission a success.

Let us always remember how much Śrīla Prabhupāda desired that this movement be successful. There have been, are, and will be discrepancies and difficulties within ISKCON, especially without Prabhupāda to personally scold us and keep us in order. We sometimes tend to forget exactly what Śrīla Prabhupāda wanted us to do, and life in ISKCON has sometimes been unnecessarily difficult. Yet despite the ups and downs, when we remember that Śrīla Prabhupāda considers ISKCON nondifferent from himself, we then know that we must go on serving and cooperating within this movement to try to make it a great success.

If we are serious to serve, then surely Śrīla Prabhupāda and Kṛṣṇa will guide us. Śrīla Prabhupāda is always with us in the form of his books and instructions. If we follow those instructions without deviation, we will never be separated from him. We will earn the blessings of Śrīla Prabhupāda and the entire *paramparā*. Backed by the power of Kṛṣṇa, Śrīla Prabhupāda, and the previous *ācāryas*, there can be no question of failure. If we but remain sincere, then certainly it is just a matter of time before our endeavors blossom and flourish. We must remain patient and not expect immediate results. These are still pioneering and formative days.

The immediate years following Śrīla Prabhupāda's physical departure from our midst are the testing ground for the Kṛṣṇa consciousness movement. How Śrīla Prabhupāda's instructions are understood and implemented by the first generations of his followers will shape the future of his mission. Misinterpretation can cause chaos—as happened in Christianity, in which early belief in vegetarianism and reincarnation was later rejected, with the result that mainstream Christianity has ever since remained divorced from the true spirit of Christ. Therefore it is incumbent on Śrīla Prabhupāda's followers to carefully grasp the essence of his teachings and not speculate or deviate in any way. If we rationalize, minimize, or simply disobey Śrīla Prabhupāda's instructions, we will wither and die.

Although the guru-*paramparā* is under Kṛṣṇa's protection—Śrīla Bhaktisiddhānta Sarasvatī Ṭhākura said that the line of Bhaktivinoda will never be stopped—if we allow *māyā* to enter, the natural development of the mission will be impeded. And without becoming overwhelmed, we should face the difficulties that *māyā* inevitably imposes. Śrīla Prabhupāda himself set the example. By dint of firm faith in Kṛṣṇa's protection, he always maintained equilibrium as he captained the ISKCON ship through one storm after another. It may be that ISKCON's problems today are no greater than they were back then, but that our ability to overcome them is now less due to our lack of full Kṛṣṇa consciousness.

Whatever the difficulties and their causes may be, followers of Śrīla Prabhupāda should always remain connected to his mission and continue to work within it as dedicated servants. They should maintain the constant endeavor to uphold and improve standards. The test of a true disciple is to bear the burden of executing the guru's orders. For followers of Śrīla Prabhupāda, this means to continue the preaching work within the organization he established. Others may invent their "own" programs, but the true disciple sticks to the service given by his guru. It is the duty of all disciplic descendants of Śrīla Prabhupāda to work within ISKCON, according to their capacity, for the deliverance of the conditioned souls.

Without becoming engulfed by problems within our society, let us push on with our work, being always confident of Kṛṣṇa's blessings. If we simply follow in Śrīla Prabhupāda's footsteps, all success is guaranteed.

If the preachers in our Kṛṣṇa consciousness movement are sincere devotees of Kṛṣṇa, Kṛṣṇa will always be with them because He is very kind and favorable to all His devotees. Just as Arjuna and Kṛṣṇa were victorious in the Battle of Kurukṣetra, this Kṛṣṇa consciousness movement will surely emerge victorious if we but remain sincere devotees of the Lord and serve the Lord according to the advice of predecessors (the Six Gosvāmīs and other devotees of the Lord). As Narottama Dāsa Ṭhākura has stated: *tāṅdera caraṇa sevi bhakta-sane vāsa, janame janame haya ei abhilāṣa.* The Kṛṣṇa consciousness devotees must always desire to remain in the society of devotees. *Bhakta-sane vāsa:* they cannot go outside the Kṛṣṇa conscious society or the movement. Within the society we must try to serve the predecessors by preaching Caitanya Mahāprabhu's cult and spreading His name and fame all over the world. If we attempt this seriously within the society, it will be successfully done. There is no question of estimating how this will happen in the mundane sense. But without a doubt, it happens by the grace of Kṛṣṇa.[20]

A Proposal

Many members of our movement are expressing dissatisfaction, and not without cause. Therefore we submit a proposal for solving all problems within our society. It is based on the understanding that pure devotional service brings immediate relief from all kinds of material distress and is the beginning of all auspiciousness. (See *The Nectar of Devotion*, chapter one) Every devotee should:

(1) read Śrīla Prabhupāda's books one to two hours daily;

(2) chant and dance together in *kīrtana*;

(3) chant the holy names very carefully and with great attention.

Then all of us will quickly become pure devotees, will drown in an ocean of bliss, and will find that all our problems have also been drowned. Or even if difficulties remain—after all, this world was designed to be problematic—when Kṛṣṇa is pleased by our sincere efforts to serve Him, then He will definitely bless us with the realization to overcome problems, or at least learn to live with them. Purity is the force.

Feeling for Prabhupāda

It is essential that every member of ISKCON feel a strong, close bond of affection to Śrīla Prabhupāda. Certainly he feels for us, his children and grandchildren. If we are to develop genuine love, we must reciprocate with him and feel his kindness. That is what Kṛṣṇa consciousness is all about: "*Bhakti* means love. Without love there is no question of *bhakti*."[21]

It is not sufficient to go on mechanically as if Kṛṣṇa consciousness were simply some humdrum formula. We need to open our hearts and actually develop love for Kṛṣṇa, love for His devotees, and love for all living beings. To do that, we must connect with Prabhupāda, who is an ocean of love. We connect with Prabhupāda through his books and instructions. Śrīla Prabhupāda wanted his followers to read his books, so it is required that we do so, but not ritualistically, simply as a duty; loving feelings must also be developed. We may doubt, "How can we develop such feeling if we never met Śrīla Prabhupāda or had only very little personal association with him?" Answer: by hearing about him from those who were with him, by reading about him, by discussing his pastimes and qualities, and, most importantly, by praying, "Śrīla Prabhupāda, please help me."

We must become attached to Śrīla Prabhupāda. That is the sure way to success. *Mahat-sevāṁ dvāram āhur vimukteḥ*: "One can attain the path of liberation from material bondage only by rendering service to highly advanced spiritual personalities."[22] Becoming attached to Śrīla Prabhupāda means to become attached to hearing about him, reading his books, glorifying him, and quintessentially, following his instructions. "Following his instructions" does not mean to follow one or two of them according to our whims, but to make them our life and soul. This is the real meaning of putting Prabhupāda in the center.

I do not want to be taken as a *prākṛta-sahajiyā*, but I must say that if we do not at least sometimes shed a tear when remembering Śrīla Prabhupāda's extraordinary mercy upon us, then something is definitely wrong. Let's put it right—now, while there's still time.

Love Means to Follow

To have sentiment or feeling for Śrīla Prabhupāda is desired and required, but the real thing is to do what he says. Talk of love is easy, but the test is in following.

On a morning walk in Hyderabad, Śrīla Prabhupāda took the position of a Christian. "I love God," he said, and challenged his disciples to disprove his position. He rebutted all arguments until this one was proffered: "If you love God, why don't you do what He says?" Śrīla Prabhupāda then explained that by disregarding the Biblical injunction "Thou shalt not kill," the so-called Christians' hypocrisy was exposed.[23] Similarly, love for Śrīla Prabhupāda must be based on following his instructions. To praise Śrīla Prabhupāda is good and certainly should be done, but the real challenge is to become like him.

Remembrance of Śrīla Prabhupāda, love for Śrīla Prabhupāda, praise of Śrīla Prabhupāda, and service to Śrīla Prabhupāda must all be based on obeying Śrīla Prabhupāda. Otherwise,

such sentiments are superficial, hypocritical, and devoid of the potency to fulfil Śrīla Prabhupāda's mission of spreading Kṛṣṇa consciousness all over the world.

> If he cannot [follow after initiation], then he is cat and dog; he is not a human being. Why he should accept initiation? Let him remain a cat and dog. He promises to follow, and if he cannot follow then he is nothing but cat and dog. In the court they take promises "in the name of God," "in the name of Bible," so that means he will speak the truth. Similarly, before the fire, before Deity, before guru, before devotees, he is promising something, and if he does not follow, then he is cat and dog. He cannot advance; it is not possible. That is the distinction between cat and dog and human being. Cat and dog, they cannot promise; it is not possible. But a human being can promise. And if he keeps his promise, then he is human being; otherwise cat and dog. Word of honor. The cats and dogs, they have no sense of honor. Either you kick him or pat, he does not know what is the difference. That is cat and dog. He does not know the distinction. A human being knows what is promise, what is word of honor.[24]

> I want one student who follows my instruction. I don't want millions. *Ekaś candras tamo hanti na ca tārā-sahasraśaḥ:* "If there is one moon in the sky, that is sufficient for illumination; there is no need of millions of stars." So my position is that I want to see that at least one disciple has become pure devotee. Of course, I have got many sincere and pure devotees. That is my good luck. But I would have been satisfied if I could find out one only.[25]

Śrīla Prabhupāda's Loving Followers

To be a disciple of Śrīla Prabhupāda is really something special. Even devotees who left the mission many years ago can intrigue us with their wonderful stories of Śrīla Prabhupāda in the "early days." The good feeling that they got from Prabhupāda lives with them even now. Still, when we hear our strayed-away godbrothers and godsisters tell their Prabhupāda stories with such enthusiasm, we wonder:

"You love Prabhupāda, and Prabhupāda loves you. You are so fortunate to have had his intimate association. Whatever you did for Prabhupāda is to your eternal credit. You served wholeheartedly then, so why not now?

"Surrender to the spiritual master is not meant to be simply a youthful fling. He is our lord, birth after birth. You have done so much for Prabhupāda's mission. Will you not do more now? You belong at Prabhupāda's lotus feet and nowhere else. Śrīla Prabhupāda wants you. He is waiting for you. We also, your eternal spiritual relations, are missing your association and friendship. Please come and join with us again."

There are many Prabhupāda disciples, and also granddisciples, who are still devotees at some level but are spoiling their life by not practicing Kṛṣṇa consciousness seriously. Such a great asset of knowledge, experience, and advancement is going to waste! You can immensely please Śrīla Prabhupāda and help relieve the suffering of the world if you simply resume what you are meant for: giving to others what Śrīla Prabhupāda gave to you. Fellow devotees, we beg you: please return and help push on this movement in whatever capacity you can. Or at least again practice Kṛṣṇa consciousness seriously, for your own benefit and to honor your promise to Śrīla Prabhupāda. Do not neglect the valuable gift you have received. Help yourself and others by being Kṛṣṇa conscious.

My dear godbrothers and godsisters, please hear my humble request. You are all highly exalted souls. Śrīla Prabhupāda traversed the world, gathering members to his flock, and you were among the few who first responded. On his order, you sacrificed everything and took all risks to preach. How sweet and fresh were those early days!

But what about today? Let us look into our heart. Do we still cry for Prabhupāda? If not, why not? Have we become stuffy, staid, comfortable, or complacent? Are we now self-righteous senior citizens, slowly ticking on to our next change of body? Or worse still, have we slipped from the vows we made to Śrīla Prabhupāda?

Prabhus, our duty to Śrīla Prabhupāda is not over. It is not enough simply to remember him fondly. We must do some significant service. The Kṛṣṇa consciousness movement did not end in 1977. There is so much to be done all over the world. So many devotees need the association of experienced, mature devotees. As senior family members, we must help the newer devotees, even if due to their inexperience they do not always treat us as they should.

Whatever bliss we experienced in the "Prabhupāda days" can be had again, for those days are not, nor ever will be, over. "Śrīla Prabhupāda lives forever by his divine instructions, and the follower lives with him." If we are not feeling the bliss of Kṛṣṇa consciousness, we cannot blame it on any external cause. Śrīla Prabhupāda has given us everything. He gave us the nectar of serving Kṛṣṇa in ISKCON. The nectar is still there. It is up to us to again become properly linked.

Śrīla Prabhupāda was sometimes quite frank about his followers: "I am engaging fools, rascals—anyone—to spread Kṛṣṇa consciousness."[26] "We have to select men from the worst class, those who were finished, tenth class."[27] Prabhupāda once compared himself to Lord Rāma, who had crossed the ocean to bring Lakṣmī from the hands of the demons back to India, and said, "Just as Lord Rāma had an army of monkeys to help Him, so do I."

Of course, Śrīla Prabhupāda loved his monkeys and encouraged their unsophisticated attempts to become worthy members of the Gauḍīya Vaiṣṇava *sampradāya.* He never forgot any sincere service rendered by any disciple. Although stern in his admonishment, he was ever ready to forgive an errant disciple and encourage him to continue in devotional service. Although fully aware of his disciples' failings, only in a few rare cases, only if a disciple had become consciously offensive, did Śrīla Prabhupāda actually reject any disciple.

Śrīla Prabhupāda not only loved his monkeys but was proud of them and praised their astounding feats in preaching Kṛṣṇa consciousness. Let us still today encourage one another and offer tribute to devotees who continue to excel in Śrīla Prabhupāda's service. Although one rather glum outlook is to downplay the glorifying of Śrīla Prabhupāda's disciples, as if that somehow or other diminishes Prabhupāda's glories, actually the opposite is true: if the son is glorified, the father is automatically glorified along with him.

True, Śrīla Prabhupāda was magnificently unique. Nor had we ever before seen such a person, nor even imagined that there could be such a person. Nor have we since seen anyone who is anywhere near Śrīla Prabhupāda's stature (notwithstanding the shenanigans of assorted wannabes), nor do we expect that anyone else of that standing will appear any time soon. Personalities as great as Śrīla Prabhupāda are extremely few, and rarely do they come to this world. So it is unreasonable to deprecate the followers of Śrīla Prabhupāda for not being as great as he. Those who undeviatingly follow him share in his greatness. By his grace, they also may be glorified. Rather than searching for whatever qualities they may lack, let us try to appreciate the extraordinary mercy they have received from Śrīla Prabhupāda—the mercy to carry on his mission, according to their individual capacity. Let us remember the Vaiṣṇava spirit that Śrīla Prabhupāda taught us, and look for qualities, not faults, in devotees.

True Followers of Śrīla Prabhupāda

How do we recognize a true follower of Śrīla Prabhupāda? By his qualities. Śrīla Bhaktisiddhānta Sarasvatī Ṭhākura was acclaimed as the "lion guru," and Śrīla Prabhupāda was similarly ferocious in preaching. Lions do not give birth to lambs. The world is full of impersonalism, atheism, wickedness, and nastiness. Śrīla Prabhupāda fought constantly and untiringly against such rascaldom. If we really want to be known as followers of Śrīla Prabhupāda, we must join together and fight against all this nonsense.

Śrīla Prabhupāda wanted his followers to be preachers. Preaching is and always will be the essence. The topmost perfection for a devotee is to engage in activities to help others come back to Kṛṣṇa. Conversely, if we do not endeavor to spread Kṛṣṇa consciousness, we will simply slide into frustration and mediocrity. Let us recall those glorious days of little concern for our own comfort, of doing whatever it took to please Śrīla Prabhupāda. Those days are not historically frozen; they are here right now. They exist in the guiding words of our spiritual master. Those days are the spiritual birthright of anyone who genuinely wants them. Those days can be these days if we want them to be.

As Śrīla Prabhupāda wrote about his own guru, Śrīla Bhaktisiddhānta Sarasvatī Gosvāmī Mahārāja: "He lives forever by his divine instructions and the follower lives with him."[28]

ISKCON Fashions

The "dedicated followers of fashion" within ISKCON are always introducing new fads, which last for some time and are soon forgotten with the advent of a new craze. Some devotees are always running here and there—anxious to do this, try that, read another book, hear something different, check out a fresh experience, introduce something novel—without realizing what a valuable treasure they have: the instructions of Śrīla Prabhupāda. Better just stick to the essence, that is, what Śrīla Prabhupāda has given us. As followers of Śrīla Prabhupāda and Caitanya Mahāprabhu, the essence of our spiritual life is preaching. Our central activities are to daily chant sixteen rounds of the Hare Kṛṣṇa *mahā-mantra,* daily attend the morning program of *sādhana,* dress as devotees, eat only Kṛṣṇa-*prasāda,* and be loyal to the ISKCON institution. No need for any speculative innovations. Let us stick to the basics—"Chant Hare Kṛṣṇa and be happy."

> You must see that they strictly follow the regulative principles, the four prohibitions, as well as the devotional practices of arising early, taking morning bath, putting on *tilaka,* attending *maṅgala-ārati,* chanting *japa* sixteen rounds, and attending *Śrīmad-Bhāgavatam* class. This is the duty of all my initiated disciples, whether they are big or they are small.[29]

> Everyone must rise early, take bath, attend *maṅgala-ārati,* chant at least sixteen good rounds, attend class, and follow the four regulative principles. If these things are lax, then there is no question of spiritual life. Anyone who does not accept these things staunchly will have to fall down. You must teach them by your own personal example; otherwise how will they learn?[30]

> I am requesting again and again that all of my disciples simply follow all of the rules and regulations very strictly. Rising early,

chanting sixteen rounds, attending *maṅgala-ārati* and class, etc., are all essential for spiritual development.[31]

Getting Śrīla Prabhupāda's Mercy

Śāstra states that only the most pious and fortunate can take to devotional service. Considering this, a devotee once asked Śrīla Prabhupāda that since his disciples were previously almost all wretched, unfortunate, and devoid of pious activities, how could they have received the opportunity to serve Kṛṣṇa? Śrīla Prabhupāda retorted, "I have made your pious activities."[32]

Śrīla Prabhupāda came to spread good fortune to the world. All who came in contact with His Divine Grace were tremendously benefited, even if most were not aware of it. His family members, who lived intimately with him for so long, could hardly recognize their great fortune. Nor could the staid travelers in airports understand what benefit was accruing to them simply by their being present amid dozens of shiny-faced devotees unrestrainedly roaring "Hare Kṛṣṇa" to greet the saffron-silk swami. But Allen Ginsberg appreciated Śrīla Prabhupāda. So did Sally Agarwal. And so did the hippies, dancing with him in the park. Śrīla Prabhupāda's disciples certainly appreciated him in a most substantial manner. They shed tears for him and gave their youth to push on his mission.

Hundreds and thousands of people saw Śrīla Prabhupāda as he strode across the globe, and a few even got the precious chance to speak with him. Even today, millions throughout the world come in contact with Śrīla Prabhupāda through his books and his movement. All are fortunate, but the really fortunate are those who take advantage of that fortune by surrendering to Śrīla Prabhupāda's instructions.

Service to the *saṅkīrtana* mission is the qualification for receiving Śrīla Prabhupāda's mercy. Whether one is a disciple or a granddisciple, a congregational member or in some other category, and no matter the time or place, anyone serving this mission will be personally recognized by Śrīla Prabhupāda and receive his shelter. Thus no one should feel bereft of Śrīla Prabhupāda's association. We need only to do our best to fulfil his mission.

On Fulfilling Śrīla Prabhupāda's Desires

> Satisfaction of the self-realized spiritual master is the secret of advancement in spiritual life.

This dictum, cited by Śrīla Prabhupāda in his purport to verse 4.34 of the *Bhagavad-gītā,* formed the basis of his approach to Kṛṣṇa consciousness and his attitude toward his own guru. He also communicated this vital principle to us, thus providing a simple formula for harmonizing and channeling all our devotional activities: we must endeavor to please Śrīla Prabhupāda.

Once an ISKCON sannyasi asked a group of devotees, "Are you ready for death?" He let them consider for a few moments and then asked them again, one at a time. A few hazarded "Maybe," but most in that large group were certain—"No!" Finally, the sannyasi stated his own case: "I'm not ready to die. I first have to do something for Śrīla Prabhupāda."

Everyone should ask himself, "What am I doing for Śrīla Prabhupāda? Is it enough? Can I do more? What should I be doing that I'm not?"

What does Śrīla Prabhupāda want? He had many Kṛṣṇa conscious desires, which he wanted his followers to help him fulfil. He wanted his disciples to become pure devotees and preach the message of Kṛṣṇa to others. Both by example and precept, he emphasized preaching.

> Let us do something which will bring a peaceful revolution to the whole human society.[33]

> Let the whole United States become Vaiṣṇavas; then everyone else in the whole world will follow. That is my real ambition.[34]

Śrīla Prabhupāda said that his one problem was that he could not think small, only big. His ambitions for spreading Kṛṣṇa consciousness were enormous and mind-boggling. What can we do to actualize them? How much capability do we have? Our own strength is very limited. Sometimes we find it difficult just to maintain the minimum standard instituted by Śrīla Prabhupāda, what to speak of expanding the preaching. Nonetheless, if a devotee sincerely tries to execute the order of the spiritual master, strength will come and amazing things will happen. Despite all our shortcomings, somehow or other Śrīla Prabhupāda has chosen us, the members of the International Society for Krishna Consciousness, to fulfil his ambitions for furthering Lord Caitanya's mission. It is a great blessing to be an instrument in the hands of Śrīla Prabhupāda for changing the world by *saṅkīrtana*. All ISKCON devotees want to please Śrīla Prabhupāda, and the sure way to do that is to strive together to make his mission a great success.

Śrīla Prabhupāda told us that the only question he ever asked of his guru-mahārāja was "How can I serve you?" Now, several years after Prabhupāda's apparent departure from this world, there is sometimes confusion and disagreement over how we should best serve him: "What does Śrīla Prabhupāda want of us? What must we do now to please him?" The answer is simple, for Śrīla

Prabhupāda openly expressed his desire that there be a world revolution of Kṛṣṇa consciousness. Although book distribution is the prime program for effecting such a change, preaching must be expanded on all fronts—regular public chanting of *harināma,* mass *prasāda* distribution, dynamic programs to recruit devotees, vibrant temples with strong devotees strictly following *sādhana-bhakti,* and *daiva-varṇāśrama-dharma* self-sufficient farm communities.

What we need to do is clear, but the means for accomplishing it sometimes elicits different opinions among Śrīla Prabhupāda's followers. Sometimes Śrīla Prabhupāda would say that a particular program is the most important; other times he would emphasize another. While there is no doubt that he especially promoted distribution of his books, still, when an enthusiastic book distributor asked Śrīla Prabhupāda, "What pleases you most?" expecting the reply "Distribute my books," Śrīla Prabhupāda simply said, "If you love Kṛṣṇa."[35]

Even more vital than building temples or making much propaganda is that we become pure devotees. After all, other religious figures in history have also established worldwide institutions, erected impressive buildings, and attracted many followers. Quantitatively or externally, their achievements may compare with or even exceed those of Śrīla Prabhupāda's, but qualitatively they did not even come close. Only a pure devotee can produce pure devotees. Indeed, only Śrīla Prabhupāda has produced so many genuine candidates for pure devotional service—and from the most unlikely source. That is not to detract from the significance of expanding the Kṛṣṇa consciousness movement by all practical means, or to suggest that advancement in devotional service should be attempted apart from the standard process of participating within the *saṅkīrtana* movement. But we must maintain the proper focus.

राधेश्याम

We know what Prabhupāda said and did and what he wanted. We may not know the intricacies of why he spoke and acted as he did, but we know with certainty that he intensely loved Kṛṣṇa and wanted us also to love Kṛṣṇa. Everything he taught us, everything he requested of us, was meant to bring us to that point. Prabhupāda loved Kṛṣṇa so much that he gave his last drop of blood so that as many *jīvas* as he could reach might at least get a start in Kṛṣṇa consciousness. And he wanted his followers to advance to the highest level. If we simply follow Śrīla Prabhupāda without speculating, then by his grace we can indeed rise to that plane.

But it may take time. The best thing to offer Śrīla Prabhupāda will not be the easiest to achieve. Whatever "big" feats we may perform in devotional service, the real offering to the spiritual master is a clean heart, free from even the slightest subtle trace of material desire, a heart pure and radiant with love of Kṛṣṇa.

> I only want that all you, my disciples, always think of Kṛṣṇa and never forget Him for a moment.[36]

"What is the difficulty?" Śrīla Prabhupāda would say. Although occasionally he would point out his position as a special messenger of God, Prabhupāda never claimed any unique divinity—"Whatever I am doing you can do." Indeed, if what he had come to teach were impossible to attain, then what point would there have been to his coming? Still, although it is not intrinsically difficult to become a fully surrendered servant of the pure devotee, it might seem that not many have attained that position.

Śrīla Bhaktisiddhānta Sarasvatī Ṭhākura had only one disciple who fully understood his mission. Śrīla Prabhupāda also said, "I am the only single person preaching that Kṛṣṇa is God. No one appreciates or understands, not even my disciples."[37]

Nevertheless, although it is very difficult to understand Kṛṣṇa and His pure devotees or to follow them in full purity, we need not feel discouraged. We should go on serving them, confident that if we are sincere, they will surely help us. Realization comes by following, and following is realization.

Higher Realizations

Some devotees become enamored by sadhus with "higher realizations," who regularly speak about confidential Vṛndāvana-*līlās* in an intimate, enticing manner. Such devotees seem to think that Śrīla Prabhupāda had a lower realization because he almost always spoke the simple, basic philosophy of Kṛṣṇa consciousness and was reticent about speaking on esoteric subjects, such as the subtleties of *rasa-tattva*. However, to simply speak about "high topics" does not constitute the highest realization, which is to sacrifice everything to serve Kṛṣṇa as He wants. Kṛṣṇa wants *pṛthivīte āche yata nagarādi grāma, sarvatra pracāra haibe mora nāma*—preaching in every town and village.

Śrīla Prabhupāda was always absorbed in preaching Kṛṣṇa consciousness, presenting it at a philosophical level accessible to all. Therefore some have concluded that Śrīla Prabhupāda was a "lesser guru" who taught only at a lower level. Maybe such persons have not heard that even higher than *mādhurya*, the sweet exchange between Kṛṣṇa and the *gopīs* in Vṛndāvana, is *audārya*, the mood of liberal distribution of Kṛṣṇa-*bhakti* exhibited by Lord Caitanya. But even considering *mādhurya-rasa*, what is the essence of that *mādhurya*? To sacrifice everything for Kṛṣṇa, as did the *gopīs*. No one else of Śrīla Prabhupāda's generation sacrificed even a millionth the degree that he did.

Others may speak of *prema*, but Śrīla Prabhupāda practically demonstrated his *prema* by traveling throughout the world preaching and convincing atheists and demons that Kṛṣṇa is God—or at least taking them on. Others may talk of *prema*, but they have little potency or taste for combating atheists. They are on such a "high" level that they can hardly condescend to "come down" among the nondevotees. They may attract many followers, but mostly only persons who have already taken up devotional service. In this way, they collect sentimental sycophants who discuss esoteric teachings of the previous *ācāryas* as if to evince that they themselves are very learned and qualified. But in the opinion of Śrīla Bhaktivinoda Ṭhākura, a major requisite of a true Vaiṣṇava is his capacity to infuse *bhakti* in others.[38] Therefore, preaching—infusing *bhakti* in others—is the highest realization, and Śrīla Prabhupāda had it. In this world there is no one more dear to Kṛṣṇa than Śrīla Prabhupāda, nor will there ever be one more dear.[39]

Svavaśa Dāsa recalls Śrīla Prabhupāda's emphasizing active preaching over esoteria:

> We were on a morning walk [Detroit, 1975], and the devotees were consistently asking Śrīla Prabhupāda questions about the *gopīs*, their love for Kṛṣṇa, and intimate dealings. It seemed it was a subject matter that Śrīla Prabhupāda did not want to get into very much. It even appeared as if he was getting a little annoyed that the devotees continued to ask these questions about the *gopīs* and their relationship with Kṛṣṇa.
>
> The morning walk continued in this way for some time, and I had constantly been thinking what I could say to please Śrīla Prabhupāda. I'm sure other devotees were thinking like this too. We were all eager for his attention. At one point, when we turned around to go back to the parked cars, I was filled with so much intensity as to what I could say to Śrīla Prabhupāda, something to show some appreciation for him. I was scared,

shy—so many things—but finally I said, "Prabhupāda!" When I said his name, somehow Prabhupāda just stopped and looked right at me. I said, "Śrīla Prabhupāda, I'm a book distributor in Chicago. We are distributing so many of your books there. Our desire is to really please you by this book distribution in Chicago. Our desire is to somehow or other be able to distribute a hundred books each and every day for your satisfaction." And Prabhupāda just looked at me. I was practically in a state of shock. I could barely get these words out; my throat was choked up. I was shaking. But I felt I just had to say this to Śrīla Prabhupāda. I wanted to remember that I had said something to Prabhupāda in this lifetime.

All of a sudden, he broke out into a huge smile. He then said, "Just see. This is my real disciple. My real disciple is always thinking how to please the spiritual master, and he realizes how to please me is to distribute these books. This is an example of a real devotee." He kept telling me how nice it was that I had this desire, and how pleased he was by the book distribution in Chicago. He continued to smile, and concluded by saying, "Thank you very much!"[40]

Śrīla Prabhupāda's Dependence on His Guru

Śrīla Prabhupāda was a *nitya-siddha mahā-bhāgavata* sent by Kṛṣṇa from the spiritual world to save us all. He was so bold and convinced that he took on the whole world for Kṛṣṇa. In one sense he did not need a guru, because he was always perfect, never forgot Kṛṣṇa, and was never in illusion. Yet he always felt himself to be totally dependent on the mercy of his spiritual master.

> My spiritual master was no ordinary spiritual master. He saved me.[41]

> So somehow or other it has begun, the blessings of Bhaktisiddhānta Sarasvatī Ṭhākura, as he wanted me, he desired me. I am not very expert or educated or nothing extraordinary. But only thing is that I believed in his word. You can say that is my qualification. I believed cent percent in his word. So whatever success is there, it is just due to my firm faith in his instruction.[42]

Śrīla Prabhupāda's dependence on his guru was not simply a show to teach us. It was a deeply felt realization on the highest level of spiritual exchange, so confidential that when a devotee tried to induce Śrīla Prabhupāda to talk about it, he was cut off: "That is not your business!"[43]

Repaying Our Debt

एतदेव हि सच्छिष्यैः कर्तव्यं गुरुनिष्कृतम् ।
यद्वै विशुद्धभावेन सर्वार्थात्मार्पणं गुरौ ॥

etad eva hi sac-chiṣyaiḥ kartavyaṁ guru-niṣkṛtam
yad vai viśuddha-bhāvena sarvārthātmārpaṇaṁ gurau

> This indeed is the duty of all true disciples: to repay the debt to their spiritual master by offering him, with pure hearts, their wealth and even their very lives.[44]

> **Devotee:** How can we repay you?
>
> **Prabhupāda:** You don't require to repay. (Chuckles) I am not giving you anything. It is Kṛṣṇa's property. You repay to Kṛṣṇa. Chant Hare Kṛṣṇa and He will be repaid. Nobody can repay. Therefore it is better to remain always obliged. That's all. That's alright? Chant Hare Kṛṣṇa.[45]

> A Vaiṣṇava always feels himself incapable to repay his debt to his spiritual master; therefore he works very hard in order to try and repay that debt. He knows that without the mercy of the

KRṢNA
A.C. Bhaktivedanta Swami
KRṢNA

spiritual master one cannot preach this Kṛṣṇa consciousness, and therefore he always tries to act in such a way that he may please his guru.[46]

Actually you are correct; it is not possible for the disciple to repay the debt to the spiritual master. Therefore the disciple remains eternally indebted to the spiritual master and continually works in such a way that the spiritual master may become pleased upon him for such sincere services rendered. Always follow the four principles, take *prasādam*, and above all chant your sixteen rounds a day, and thus you will make steady advancement in devotional service. Continue to preach this movement all over the world and thus you will become happy and you will make others happy also.[47]

If you feel at all indebted to me then you should preach vigorously like me. That is the proper way to repay me. Of course, no one can repay the debt to the spiritual master, but the spiritual master is very much pleased by such an attitude by the disciple. In the *Bhagavad-gītā* it is said *vyavasāyātmikā buddhir ekeha kuru-nandana:* "Those who are on this path are resolute in purpose, and their aim is one." Our only business is to be fixed up in devotional service by pleasing the spiritual master. Those who are not fixed up, they have various lines of action. (*Eka* means "one" and *bahu* means "many.")

The real ocean of mercy is Kṛṣṇa, and it is the duty of the spiritual master to tell his disciple to come to the ocean and be happy. The spiritual master's duty is to lead the disciple to this ocean. I am trying my best and if you try to follow surely you will benefit.

Bhaktivinoda Ṭhākura has sung, *kṛṣṇa se tomāra kṛṣṇa dite pāra tomāra śakati ache/ āmi ta' kāṅgāla kṛṣna kṛṣna boli dhāi tava pāche pāche:* "Kṛṣṇa is yours and you have the power to give Him to anyone you wish. I am poor and wretched and running behind you shouting 'Kṛṣṇa! Kṛṣṇa!'"

Kṛṣṇa is unlimited—no one can catch Him—but if someone follows the *paramparā*, He agrees to be captured. Everyone is afraid of Kṛṣṇa, but Kṛṣṇa is afraid of Mother Yaśodā. That is Kṛṣṇa's special mercy.[48]

Not Just Another Guru

Vyāsa-*pūjā* offering by Jayādvaita Swami (1995)

Today we honor the representative of Śrīla Vyāsa. Śrīla Vyāsadeva has many representatives. And so we may think of Śrīla Prabhupāda as one of them. And of course he is.

Yet Śrīla Prabhupāda stands distinct, distinguished, in a class by himself. He is not merely "a guru," our guru, one among many, just as the *Bhāgavatam* is not just another book, Hare Kṛṣṇa not just another mantra, and Lord Kṛṣṇa not just another god.

To study Śrīla Prabhupāda is to study superexcellence. Part of his superexcellence is that he did act just as though "another guru." He did things any guru should do, or at least aspire to; he set an example for us to follow. (Harikeśa Mahārāja has written about this very nicely for the Vyāsa-*pūjā* of a previous year.)

Yet Śrīla Prabhupāda also did the extraordinary, and was extraordinary. And we need to keep his singularity in mind.

Some people, it seems, suppose that any guru, to be bona fide, must come up to the same level, or nearly the same, as Śrīla Prabhupāda. But that is neither necessary nor possible.

It is not necessary because Śrīla Prabhupāda far excelled the qualifications every bona fide guru must have. There may be many fragrant flowers, but among them there is extraordinary excellence in the *campaka* or the rose; there may be many birds, but among them special excellence in the peacock or the swan; many stars, but among them special excellence in the moon.

Among gurus, Śrīla Prabhupāda shines with extraordinary brilliance. To expect that sort of brilliance from every guru is to expect the impossible—and to lose sight of how extraordinary Śrīla Prabhupāda is.

Then again, if by virtue of serving as guru one thinks one has become as good as Prabhupāda, or nearly so, again one has lost one's vision. We've had our experience: the little mice who became tigers and cast hungry eyes on the yogi turned into little mice again.

Śrīla Prabhupāda stood in a class apart, uniquely blessed by Śrīla Bhaktisiddhānta Sarasvatī Ṭhākura and Śrī Caitanya Mahāprabhu to establish Kṛṣṇa consciousness all over the world. Anyone who wants to cover the same territory, take on the same task, but not follow in Śrīla Prabhupāda's footsteps, is an offender and a fool. And anyone who sincerely dedicates his life to Śrīla Prabhupāda's service will always come out successful, overcoming even the most subtle and difficult obstacles.

This year at Māyāpur, Kṛṣṇa reaffirmed to us the depth and purity of Śrīla Prabhupāda's teachings. When Śrīla Prabhupāda conveyed to us conclusions of the previous *ācāryas*, he did so perfectly, preserving and transmitting the philosophy exactly as it is, neither watering anything down, nor covering anything over, nor leaving anything out. He gave us the essence of everything, exactly as we ought to receive it.

We therefore don't need to add anything, subtract anything, or change anything. We need only faithfully serve Śrīla Prabhupāda's orders, and everything will be revealed.

Hare Kṛṣṇa.

Founder-Ācārya

The following is a GBC resolution, passed in 1994:

That the following statement be accepted as ISKCON's statement about the founder-*ācārya:*

To fulfil the previous *ācāryas'* desire for a united worldwide preaching organization to expand Śrī Caitanya Mahāprabhu's mission, Śrīla Prabhupāda founded the International Society for Krishna Consciousness as a distinct branch of the Brahmā-Mādhva-Gauḍīya-Vaiṣṇava *sampradāya.* Therefore he is the founder-*ācārya* of ISKCON.

(a) Śrīla Prabhupāda is the foundational *śikṣā-guru* for all ISKCON devotees because he has realized and presented the teachings of the previous *ācāryas* of the Brahmā-Mādhva-Gauḍīya *sampradāya* appropriately for the modern age.

(b) Śrīla Prabhupāda's instructions are the essential teachings for every ISKCON devotee.

(c) Śrīla Prabhupāda's books are the embodiment of his teachings and should be accepted as the standard by all future generations of ISKCON.

(d) Śrīla Prabhupāda should be worshiped daily by every ISKCON member.

(e) Every ISKCON spiritual master is responsible to guide his disciples to follow Śrīla Prabhupāda's instructions.

(f) As founder-*ācārya,* Śrīla Prabhupāda gave directions for management, principles of cooperation, and other practical guidelines which form the basis and inspiration for ISKCON's policies.

(g) Śrīla Prabhupāda established the Governing Body Commission to execute his will, following the order of the previous *ācāryas*.

Vyāsa-pūjā Offerings

1980

(Submitted on behalf of ISKCON Dacca)

Dear Śrīla Prabhupāda,

Again on your Vyāsa-*pūjā* day we gladly take extra time from the duties you have given us to meditate deeply on your personality and the purpose of your mission.

How strange, the materialists will say, that we are making offerings to a person long since departed. Such sweet sentimentalism must be a fascination within the mind.

But no. Unlike material relationships, which are terminated by death, this relationship is deathless—and not just in name, nor simply as a philosophical theory.

Rather, the mature disciple sees with the eye of eternity. "I am eternal, my spiritual master is eternal, and he is inviting me to develop an eternal reciprocation of service and instruction." Why? For the pleasure of the supreme eternal, Śrī Kṛṣṇa.

This *rasa* is not limited by respective positions in time and space. It is based on the consciousness—the serving mood—of the disciple, who is engaged by the perfect spiritual master, the pure devotee of Kṛṣṇa. It is solidified by the sincere determination of the disciple to continue acting as he is instructed by his *paramahaṁsa*-guru.

Śrīla Prabhupāda, your activities are certainly mysterious. We never believed that you would leave us here when we were still so inexperienced. You left this world still unknown to its masses, before the Kṛṣṇa consciousness movement's full glory was established.

We have heard that for your early disciples, to print and distribute a few BTGs seemed like a momentous task.* But you had given the order, and you provided the inspiration, the determination, and the know-how to make it possible. The same disciples who stayed faithful to your lotus feet now lead us in pushing, pushing, pushing on the message of Śrī Caitanya Mahāprabhu.

New frontiers open, more *bhaktas* come, problems arise and are solved—the Kṛṣṇa consciousness movement expands. The future is unavoidable. The Hare Kṛṣṇa movement is becoming huge, auspicious, and all-successful. And we, your disciples who a few days ago didn't know how to hold a broom, must accept responsibility—responsibility for preaching, for book translation, publication and distribution, for training *bhaktas*, for improved standards, for favorable public opinion, for internal purity, and for gorgeous Deity worship.

In the face of this enormous task, we feel ourselves utterly helpless. To you, the spiritual master without whom we wouldn't even know what *tilaka* is, we offer our most grateful thanks. We can do wonderful things—but only if we pray to you, taking the position of menial servants and never becoming puffed up.

Śrīla Prabhupāda, we know that you have not left us, because you are manifest in the hearts and activities of your most sincere disciples. You have given us the ISKCON *ācāryas*, and they in turn are giving you to the world.

We pray that we may become ever conscious of your desire to bring everyone to Kṛṣṇa's lotus feet. We pray for the strength

---

* BTG—*Back to Godhead* magazine.

to throw off all petty material desires and to be fixed as your eternal surrendered servants. We beg for the mercy to chant your name and dance like madmen: *Jaya* Prabhupāda! *Jaya* Prabhupāda! *Jaya* Prabhupāda!

In millions of lifetimes we cannot thank you enough for what you have done for us; therefore we simply offer ourselves at your lotus feet.

Your disciples in Bangladesh.

1981

(Submitted on behalf of ISKCON Bangladesh)

nama oṁ viṣṇu-pādāya kṛṣṇa-preṣṭhāya bhū-tale
śrīmate bhaktivedānta-svāminn iti nāmine
namas te sārasvate deve gaura-vāṇī-pracāriṇe
nirviśeṣa-śūnyavādi-pāścātya-deśa-tāriṇe

Dear Śrīla Prabhupāda,

With great pleasure we again take the opportunity to write in praise of you for your Vyāsa-*pūjā* offering. Actually, we should be offering at every moment words in glorification of your activities, and there is no limit to such praises. But we feel that our words, however nicely composed, shall stand hollow without the real feeling that is meant to give them substance. O Lord Kṛṣṇa, at least this once, let our hearts fill with sincerity so that we may properly praise Your pure devotee. (Here stands a dilemma. Whatever we write is certain to be full of all the base qualities of which we are made, and even if externally it seems to be purely motivated, Śrīla Prabhupāda can see right through to all the rubbish desires in our hearts. Maybe it would be better to offer a few simple words and the rest mentally. But no, it is our duty to praise the spiritual master. A father accepts even a valueless gift from his small child because it is offered in a spirit of love. So, although we are unfit, and our words cannot increase Śrīla Prabhupāda's greatness, still we must write.)

O Śrīla Prabhupāda, your presence is always keenly felt by us in everything that we do that you have given to us—in your taped lectures and *kīrtanas*, in your books and instructions, in the morning program, in *prasāda*, in preaching, and now in *Śrīla Prabhupāda-līlāmṛta*.

Therefore it is still a shock to us sometimes when we suddenly realize that you are no longer personally present with us. Like birds suddenly left to fend for themselves, we feel somewhat lost.

The Māyāpur-Vṛndāvana festival will never be the same. No longer will your disciples anxiously await the next volume of your *Bhāgavatam* purports. "Where is Prabhupāda now? What wonderful activities has he now performed? What revelations has he just made?" This excited talk will never again pass through the corridors of your temples.

Still, Śrīla Prabhupāda, your great gift is to teach us that we are all eternal and are meant to serve the Supreme Eternal, Śrī Kṛṣṇa, through the grace of Śrī Śrī Gaura-Nitāi. Therefore our remembrance of you is not some sentimental sob. There is no question of simply making some poetic offering to you once a year. You are the living (yes!) eternal founder-*ācārya* of ISKCON and will always remain the center of everything. Anyone who fails to recognize this will fall away. Real sincerity is shown by a sustained effort in following your instructions, especially in preaching.

Personally, when I consider my own position, I should be very unhappy. Practically speaking, you have given us eternal life, knowledge, and bliss in the service of Śrī Kṛṣṇa—but I am such a dullhead, I am still addicted to material, ghastly things.

The spiritual master's business is to present complete knowledge of spiritual life to the disciple and to guide him on the correct path. But ultimately the disciple's sincerity in purpose in attempting to please the guru sets the rate of the disciple's progress.

On Vyāsa-*pūjā* day, we are supposed to make an offering to the *ācārya,* but considering my own position, I am again begging from you, Śrīla Prabhupāda. Please force me to engage wholeheartedly in your service. I am ashamed to admit that without such pressure I will not do so—I am such a rascal, weak-hearted.

Actually, I need you to beat on my head till I submit—but I know myself to be useless. I whimsically ask for required punishment, but when it comes, then I complain! Śrīla Prabhupāda, please have mercy on me. Certainly, my position is hopeless, but unless I am connected to you, though unfit, my existence is meaningless.

Śrīla Prabhupāda, the offenseless chanting of Hare Kṛṣṇa which you have given to us will ultimately bring one to enter the pastimes of Lord Caitanya and Lord Kṛṣṇa. Of course, I cannot aspire for such a position. Let me pray again and again that once in the coming crores of my rebirths I may at least once get your holy *darśana* and take your lotus foot dust as a decoration on my head. And if somehow or other I could become one of your intimate disciples and go universe to universe with you—that is the topmost desire of my heart.

Your disciples and granddisciples in Bangladesh.

1982

(Submitted on behalf of ISKCON Bangladesh)

Dear Śrīla Prabhupāda,

Please accept our humble obeisances. All glories to your lotus feet!

You have given us

Śrī Śrī Gaura-Nitāi

Śrī Śrī Rādhā-Govinda

Śrī Śrī Rādhā-Mādhava

Śrī Śrī Rādhā-Vṛndāvanacandra

Śrī Śrī Rādhā-Gokulānanda

Śrī Śrī Śrī Jagannātha-Subhadrā-Baladeva

and so many other worshipable forms of the Lord.

You have given us the most precious gift, pure devotional service to the holy name of the Lord.

You went amongst the *yavanas* and *mlecchas*, preached, and thus, out of the most unlikely candidates, created *sādhu-saṅga* for us: the International Society for Krishna Consciousness.

You have given us Māyāpur, Vṛndāvana, Ratha-yātrā, temples, *prasāda*, *saṅkīrtana*, farms, *tilaka*, *gurukula*, and transcendental art.

You have given us BBT (your heart), ISKCON (your body), and *lakṣmī* (your blood).

Your gifts are innumerable and still expanding.

Thank you, Śrīla Prabhupāda, for these wonderful transcendental gifts. Thank you for your eternal protection.

From your disciples and granddisciples in Bangladesh

P.S. We also have a request: now please shed a special glance of mercy on this unfortunate land, once a bastion of Vaiṣṇavism, now covered by lamentation. Wherever your message is broadcast here, immediately people become joyful; but the darkness is great, and we are but few, and weak.

1983

(Submitted on behalf of ISKCON Bangkok)

nama oṁ viṣṇu-pādāya kṛṣṇa-preṣṭhāya bhū-tale
śrīmate bhaktivedānta-svāminn iti nāmine
namas te sārasvate deve gaura-vāṇī-pracāriṇe
nirviśeṣa-śūnyavādi-pāścātya-deśa-tāriṇe

Dear Śrīla Prabhupāda,

Please accept our prostrated obeisances at your lotus feet. To find sufficient adjectives to praise you is not difficult. You are most praiseworthy, and your achievements are well known to all. So, by consulting a thesaurus, we could begin to put together a suitable essay.

But we know that literary ingenuity cannot impress you as you read these offerings. You are looking to see how much, year after year, your disciples, granddisciples, and eventually great-granddisciples, are progressing on the path back to Godhead by developing their affection for, and surrender to, your divine lotus feet.

This is our spiritual life. This has meaning. No one but the devotees can understand this sweet exchange between guru and disciple. You are the guru of gurus, the shelter of those who give shelter, the founder-*ācārya* of your own International Society for Krishna Consciousness.

Through the association of devotees in your ISKCON society, our path of spiritual progress is straightforward, pure, and simple. We are so much grateful to you for having given us the association of pure devotees in the ISKCON society.

We just want to serve you, following your program of chanting, dancing, feasting, and vigorous preaching. Although our tendency is to stray away, the austerities involved in our preaching service force us to always drag our minds back to the shelter of your fearless lotus feet. This is your mercy.

Janme janme prabhu sei—this is our greatest hope, to obtain that shelter birth after birth. Empires may come and go, the swirling, twirling illusory energy may present so much phantasmagoria before us but we desire only to remain fixed in meditation on your lotus feet—even through the calamities of death and rebirth. You are the personification of kindness. Who could be kinder than you? So kindly award that benediction to us. We are eternally grateful to you.

Your servants at ISKCON Bangkok

1984

(Submitted on behalf of ISKCON Malaysia)

nama oṁ viṣṇu-pādāya kṛṣṇa-preṣṭhāya bhū-tale
śrīmate bhaktivedānta-svāminn iti nāmine

namas te sārasvate deve gaura-vāṇī-pracāriṇe
nirviśeṣa-śūnyavādi-pāścātya-deśa-tāriṇe

Dear Śrīla Prabhupāda,

On this most important of festivals, we are simply remembering the *cintāmaṇi* magic mood of your 1965–1977 preaching *līlā*. We, the whole ISKCON society, orbited around you, and we, your disciples, danced like puppets to your direction. Your words were law, your pronunciations scripture, and your activities all-instructive *līlā*. The devotees, like bees anxious for honey, eagerly awaited your latest revelations in the form of your Bhaktivedanta purports, lecture tapes, and personal instructions.

Of course, there were big devotees and small devotees, but all were ants compared to you. After you left, we were dumbstruck, thinking, "The only pure devotee on the planet has left; what to do now?"

But, somehow, we got back into the rhythm again, by remembering your divine instructions. Several of your leading disciples have taken up the mind-boggling responsibilities of *ācārya*-ship and have done very well, by your divine grace. In fact, we are seeing your potency manifested through your advanced disciples. Thus the movement continues to expand and grow. What does the future hold? Only brightness, if we remember you, Śrīla Prabhupāda. And only darkness if we forget you or foolishly, madly, even slightly begin to relegate you to the past. You are our Kṛṣṇa conscious past; without you our present Kṛṣṇa consciousness has no meaning whatsoever, and you are also our only hope for the future.

Our only hope is always you, Śrīla Prabhupāda. ISKCON will succeed, by *your* divine grace. It's not that we've become so big that we can stand independently of you. We must always remain helpless infants before you. Then only can we be successful. Just as when you were personally present, all doubts, fears, and dissension were resolved in you, let us keep that mood now and forever. We want you to reappear again, Prabhupāda, in our hearts, manifest millions of times more strongly through our pure desire to receive you, for without you we have no hope whatsoever.

1985

(Submitted on behalf of ISKCON Bangkok)

Dear Śrīla Prabhupāda,

Please accept our humble obeisances in the dust of your lotus feet.

nama oṁ viṣṇu-pādāya kṛṣṇa-preṣṭhāya bhū-tale
śrīmate bhaktivedānta-svāminn iti nāmine
namas te sārasvate deve gaura-vāṇī-pracāriṇe
nirviśeṣa-śūnyavādi-pāścātya-deśa-tāriṇe

Our lives have become meaningful because of connection with you. We have been linked up with Kṛṣṇa only through you.

Now our ISKCON *ācāryas* are worshiped gorgeously, given the best anywhere—only because of their intimate connection with you.

Everywhere, people are eager to welcome us, because we are coming from you. In India, people line up to buy our books, because they are written by you. In our *kīrtana*, our preaching, our Deity worship, *prasāda*—everything—we see only you.

That name, fame, and glory which is so vastly due to you, but which you carefully avoided during your manifest presence, is now coming, as the people of the world wake up to your greatness.

As millions come to bow down before you in Vṛndāvana, Māyāpur, and New Vrindaban, they will look to us for guidance on the spiritual path which you first showed.

They will respect us, expecting the highest standard of spiritual competence from us, because we are the representatives of you.

When we are prepared to receive all your blessings, you will shower your mercy on us. Now let us be ready. Being ready means: *guru-mukha-padma-vākya cittete koriyā aikya.*

"World first, zone second." Our love for you will be shown by our cooperation to please you.

Formerly, there was one leader—you. Now there are many leaders. But none can be as absolute as you. You are the standard. "Leader" means simply to carry that standard.

These zones, these temples, these devotees, this *lakṣmī*—all belongs to you, Śrīla Prabhupāda. None of it is ours. We are simply your humble servants.

When pure devotees perform *saṅkīrtana,* there is no party spirit. So our continued efforts to spread the Kṛṣṇa consciousness movement will actually be successful when we all constantly consider the common benefit of worldwide ISKCON.

All glories to your lotus feet, Śrīla Prabhupāda. Let us always keep them in our hearts.

[I did not submit an offering in 1986]

1987

(Submitted on behalf of ISKCON Bangladesh)

It's Catching On, Śrīla Prabhupāda

nama oṁ viṣṇu pādāya kṛṣṇa-preṣṭhāya bhū-tale
śrīmate bhaktivedānta-svāminn iti nāmine
namas te sārasvate deve gaura-vāṇī-pracāriṇe
nirviśeṣa-śūnyavādi-pāścātya-deśa-tāriṇe

Kṛṣṇa consciousness is catching on in Bangladesh, Śrīla Prabhupāda. Of course, the Hindu population here has sustained their tremendous enthusiasm and respect for us ever since we first came. After all, the culture of East Bengal Hindus is Caitanya Vaiṣṇavism—worship of Śrī Śrī Gaura-Nitāi and Śrī Śrī Rādhā-Kṛṣṇa with *khol*, *karatālas*, and *hari-nāma saṅkīrtana*.

For eight years our traveling parties have crisscrossed this country, staging mass public festivals. Some of our devotees have become very well known, and your books are in thousands of homes. This past year we've been observing some of the effects of this work. The consciousness that, along with chanting Hare Kṛṣṇa, one should practice *sadācāra* (especially vegetarianism—sad to say, although people worship Gaurāṅga, they still mostly eat fish) is definitely growing. More and more people are coming forward for initiation. Some of the local devotees are taking up leadership roles and establishing preaching programs in different parts of the country. Śrī Puṇḍarīka Dhāma, our first Rādhā-Kṛṣṇa temple in Bangladesh, is also the first major public temple established in East Bengal in living memory. It has greatly increased the prestige of your movement here.

Now another project is beginning—Śrī Śrī Rūpa Sanātana Smṛti Tīrtha, near the site of the house built by Sanātana Gosvāmī's father, Kumāradeva, which is mentioned in *Bhakti-ratnākara* and also in one of your *Caitanya-caritāmṛta* purports. The festival programs are continuing, and book distribution is steadily increasing.

Still, there are many difficulties to overcome. There is a long, long way to go. But, by your grace, the prospects are bright. Please give us your blessings to continue this work.

Your servants in Bangladesh.
(Written by Ilāpati Dāsa)

1988

(Submitted on behalf of ISKCON Dhaka, Bangladesh)

Dear Śrīla Prabhupāda,

Please accept our humble obeisances.

> *nama oṁ viṣṇu-pādāya kṛṣṇa-preṣṭhāya bhū-tale*
> *śrīmate bhaktivedānta-svāminn iti nāmine*
> *namas te sārasvate deve gaura-vāṇī-pracāriṇe*
> *nirviśeṣa-śūnyavādi-pāścātya-deśa-tāriṇe*

Śrīla Prabhupāda, we should praise you every day, at every moment. Every morning in *maṅgala-ārati* and guru-*pūjā*, in the Gāyatrī mantras, before class or taking *prasāda*, on resting and rising, plus every time we offer obeisances, we offer you prayers—but now, under the pressure of writing a Vyāsa-*pūjā* offering, I'm having to think seriously, at last, about who you are and what you mean to us all.

Admittedly (there's no use pretending—I might be able to fool others, but I certainly can't fool you), my consciousness is dull. Therefore, to praise you, which should be the spontaneous function of the tongue, now seems like hard work. But even if reams of eloquence fell off my pen, that wouldn't fool you, either. The real guru-*pūjā* is the sincere mood of service—an offering of our lives, day after day, minute after minute.

Externally, I may appear to be doing that—after all, I'm still in the mainstream of ISKCON, which could be a cause of smugness, going by percentages. But apart from that fact, I have very little to offer you. My spiritual progress is, at best, zero. For how many years will I have to lament like this at Vyāsa-*pūjā* time? Will I have to go through many lifetimes like this?

Śrīla Prabhupāda, apart from my own rotten condition, I am also worried for the movement you gave us. ISKCON was built with your blood, sweat, and tears—but now we don't have the dynamism, mood, and sense of purpose of those "Prabhupāda's days." It's a changing movement in a changing world. Without your personal guidance we're often unsure on which path to tread. The dangers of compromise, complacency, alteration, outright deviation, and—as always—plain old sex desire, whirl and swirl like dangerous waves to rock the boats of our good intentions.

And what of the future? Even now, we fear pseudo-gurus who take your name as a masthead while propagating all kinds of nonsense to increase their own name, fame, and glory. Will we see family lines develop, with devotees claiming privilege due to the achievements of their forefathers? Will we become concerned with external formalities, forgetting the goal of life—to become mad after Kṛṣṇa? Or, worse still, adopt the philosophy that "It's OK if you don't follow the regulative principles; just be a devotee anyway."

History shows that after the disappearance of a great religious teacher, so many subsects spring up partially professing his teachings and following his practices, but all more or less deviated from the actual path he taught. Right here in Bangladesh we have to struggle against so many nonsense pseudo-Vaiṣṇavas leading people to hell in the name of Caitanya Mahāprabhu (although unfortunately some of the men within our camp are also influenced by them). *Sahajiyās, jāta-gosāis,* imitation incarnations, purveyors of "new" "*mahā*-mantras," professional kirtaneers, professional gurus, professional reciters of *Śrīmad-Bhāgavatam,* singers who "howl" (that's the term you used) in the name of chanting, in a perverse imitation of separation from Kṛṣṇa, but who follow their performance with a cigarette then go home to eat fish—you name it, we've got them all. Today Bangladesh, tomorrow the world?

We *must* follow *your* path *strictly*—otherwise we'll just be missionaries of neo-Hinduism. We must preach Kṛṣṇa consciousness as you have given it to us. We must give those joining this movement a full opportunity to develop pure Kṛṣṇa consciousness by training them to become conversant with your books and your ideas. Otherwise, in your name we'll be cheating them.

Kṛṣṇa consciousness is your gift to the world. We must live it, experience it, and give it to others. Such transcendental religion always exists far above mundane piety and moral principles. That Kṛṣṇa consciousness you have given us as it is, completely, perfect. Your spiritual master, in what would have been a lifetime's research for a lesser genius, thoroughly studied all the Vaiṣṇava traditions and methods of practice, and, with intelligence directly illuminated by Kṛṣṇa, gave us Kṛṣṇa consciousness for the modern age—"Bhakti-siddhānta." You brought that message intact to the West. If (it's almost

unthinkable) you hadn't come, then cats, dogs, and monkeys as we were, we would never have had a chance to know of Kṛṣṇa or to save ourselves from hell. You presented one-hundred-percent genuine Kṛṣṇa consciousness in such a palatable way as to be attractive to those whom others—big godbrothers and scholars—never cared to give a chance to. The results were wonderful. That we made such a mess of it doesn't take a glimmer off your glories. Rather, it serves to clarify the difference between a real *ācārya* and any dozens of imitation glowworms.

So we've got the perfect package from you, and though we may research into the history of our *sampradāya,* translate the words of our *sampradāya-ācāryas,* and even write our own books (none of which are outside your mandate), still, we must always remember that your books are the lawbooks for ISKCON, and that your way of doing things is our way of doing things. We have no access to any aspects of Kṛṣṇa consciousness except through the understanding and path you have given us.

Sometimes great *ācāryas* appear to say contradictory things, or teach Kṛṣṇa consciousness in different ways and on different levels according to time, place, and circumstance. However, there need be no misunderstanding—you are our *ācārya* (founder-*ācārya* of ISKCON—the *sampradāya-ācārya* for ten thousand years). What you say is *śāstra.* Kṛṣṇa is directly speaking through you. "If you think I have made a mistake, you have made a mistake." If anyone goes outside your teachings or practices, he is to be rejected, that's all. No confusion, no Frogism. This is the way of *ācāryas. Yasya deve parā bhaktiḥ…*

Our only hope—as always—is your instructions. Clear, simple, and direct, your words are Vaikuṇṭha-*kathā,* which stab through all material coverings and enter the hearts of receptive devotees.

Śrīla Prabhupāda, we are struggling. In our hearts, we really desire to surrender to you, but we are compromised by *māyā*. After so many years, we have no better prayer to you than to please force your way into our minds, and drag us, even though we resist, to the lotus feet of your beloved Kṛṣṇa. If it wasn't for Vyāsa-*pūjā*, I wouldn't have thought to say all these things, but now I have been forced to write, I realize that, after all, my heart's desire is to serve you.

This is a very personalized offering, but anyway, I'm offering it on behalf of the devotees here in Bangladesh. Considering the circumstances, your movement had done fairly well here, though there are definitely vast improvements needed in some areas. My promise to you is that, while I'm in Bangladesh, I'll try to get the initiated devotees at least to read your books—which they all need to do a lot more than they are presently doing.

Thank you very much for all you have given us, Śrīla Prabhupāda. Please forgive me yet again for being such a sham devotee (how many times will I have to beg for forgiveness—how many times will you forgive me?).

Praying to come alive and sometime develop attachment for your lotus feet.

On behalf of the devotees in Bangladesh, your servant,
Ilāpati Dāsa

1989

Prabhupāda-caraṇa-reṇu

Śrīla Prabhupāda, the tide is turning. Your (and our) ISKCON is again becoming more and more ecstatic every day. The most amazing news is that the apparently impenetrable bastions of the Communist powers have accepted your order. That which we dreamt of happening in some distant future is with us now: Kṛṣṇa consciousness is being practiced openly in countries which only three years ago persecuted devotees. This is proof that the inconceivable potency by which Kṛṣṇa spreads the Kṛṣṇa consciousness movement is still very much alive in ISKCON.

In the West, the preaching is continuing, and devotees are simultaneously looking inwards toward their cultural roots. Many are coming to Vṛndāvana for intensive month-long programs of studying your books. This year's Māyāpur Festival also marked a continued return to sanity, based on *śravaṇaṁ kīrtanaṁ viṣṇoḥ smaraṇaṁ pāda-sevanam*. All this is in pursuance of your order: "I am building these temples in Māyāpur and Vṛndāvana so that my Western disciples can come to India to learn about Kṛṣṇa consciousness." An annual Vraja-maṇḍala Parikramā has been started by your disciples, and a Gaura-maṇḍala Parikramā will begin next year.

All in all, life in ISKCON has steadied out. Problems are still there and always will be, but the worldwide atmosphere is becoming favorable. The next requirement is a big push on book distribution and preaching, coupled with a commitment to dissolve the *anarthas* which have entered your society. Then if we can just stay on the right track this time, we'll all be set up for dancing our way back to Godhead. It really is all your mercy, Śrīla Prabhupāda.

The history of ISKCON since your disappearance from our vision less than twelve years ago is a demonstration of the stanza you quoted so often:

yasya prasādād bhagavat-prasādo
yasyāprasādān na gatiḥ kuto 'pi

As you demonstrated in your life, even in one's darkest hours, when all seems impossible, if a devotee simply remains fixed on the principle of satisfying the spiritual master, all success is assured. On the other hand, despite having a big title, many properties, and thousands of followers, if one cannot satisfy the spiritual master, one cannot make any progress in spiritual life.

The dictum is so clear as to be frightening. The seductive witches of material desire, the attractively dressed *viṣa-kanyās* of prestige, position, and glory, are whispering us away from you to a lonely spot where they can kill us with their kisses. Śrīla Prabhupāda, save us! Fix us in the dust of your lotus feet by the strong attachment of selfless service. Somehow or other, in all that we are doing, in our *sādhana*, in our preaching, in our struggles, if we can just attain the position of an atom in the dust of your lotus feet, that will be our success, that will be our reward. We have nothing else to aspire to.

Your soft lotus feet are traveling from universe to universe, picking up millions of conditioned souls, who cling to your lotus feet as their only salvation. The members of ISKCON are all dust particles of your lotus feet and are therefore worshipable by me. Please give me an eternal place among them.

Now, by the mercy of your disciples, you have given me the order of *sannyāsa*. Please bless me to make good use of it in your service and not to become abominable by using it for comfort and false prestige.

Always desiring to bathe in the dust of your lotus feet,

Praying for the mercy to have your feet placed on my head life after life (damn any puffed-up eloquence—give me one drop of sincerity),

Your aspiring servant,
Bhakti Bikash Swami (still your Ilāpati Dāsa)

1990

If Prabhupāda Had Not Come

If Prabhupāda had not come (who can imagine?),
what would have been our position?
How could we have lived?
The science of Kṛṣṇa consciousness,
the ultimate limit of love of God ...
who would have let the world know?

From "you are not this body" to
the secret pastimes in the groves of Vṛndāvana ...
entrance requires special expertise.
Who else but Prabhupāda could have
been empowered to empower others to understand?

So, sing, sing again! The glories of Śrīla Prabhupāda,
making the heart pure and simple.
In this ocean of birth and death,
such a merciful person ...
we don't find any other.

Without singing the praises of Śrīla Prabhupāda,

how can we survive. What is the point of living?

This fallen disciple

regrets that his heart is like a stone

and wonders by what misfortune

he is not attracted to his guru's lotus feet.

Submissively offered to His Divine Grace A.C. Bhaktivedanta Swami Prabhupāda on the occasion of his Vyāsa-*pūjā* celebration, 1990, by a fallen disciple,

Bhakti-vikāśa Swami

1991

Śrī Guru Caraṇe Rati

nama oṁ viṣṇu-pādāya kṛṣṇa-preṣṭhāya bhū-tale
śrīmate bhaktivedānta-svāminn iti nāmine
namas te sārasvate deve gaura-vāṇī-pracāriṇe
nirviśeṣa-śūnyavādi-pāścātya-deśa-tāriṇe

Dear Śrīla Prabhupāda,

Please accept my humble obeisances in the dust of your lotus feet.

All glories to you, Śrīla Prabhupāda! You are our worshipable deity (SB 11.2.37, 11.3.22). ISKCON is your body, BBT is your heart, and *lakṣmī* collections are your blood. Only you cared so much for Kṛṣṇa that you "kicked on the face with boot" His imitators and detractors! ... thus not denying the dust of your triumphant lotus feet even to the demons.

śrī-guru-caraṇe rati, ei sei uttama gati
ye prasāde pūre sarva āśā

The topmost achievement in spiritual life is devotion to the lotus feet of Śrīla Prabhupāda. By his mercy all spiritual aspirations are fulfilled.

Śrīla Prabhupāda, you are the personification of Lord Caitanya's causeless mercy. Lord Caitanya wanted Kṛṣṇa consciousness spread all over the world, and you did it.

I was one of many who you picked up. I was suffering. Not a little, but a lot. Not briefly, but eternally. Being a demon, envious and mischievous, in the "lowest of men" class, I was perpetually being cast into the ocean of material existence, in various demoniac species of life. Sin and selfishness were all I knew. There was no possibility of my attaining Kṛṣṇa consciousness. Who was Kṛṣṇa? I had no knowledge of or inclination for Him. How was my wretched existence redeemed, being washed to the shore of your lotus feet? The only answer is: "causeless mercy."

You saved me. You saved all of us. It was you, no one else. You are our only hope—hope for the hopeless.

I was a street dog; you, a Vaiṣṇava aristocrat. What did you have to do with me? But you picked me up. Indeed, you did not hesitate to pick me up. Being still filled with an astonishing repertoire of ghastly material desires, I am still so far from Kṛṣṇa. I know that my lack of advancement in Kṛṣṇa consciousness cannot be very pleasing to you. But still I am not despondent, because I have got you. Now I am a dog with a master (*sanātha-jīvitam*). A dog is kickable, but somehow you haven't kicked me away yet. So I shamelessly beg you now to give me the mercy of the severe kicks of rectification, which I so badly need.

Śrīla Prabhupāda, unless you kick me into shape, how am I ever going to control my mind? Although I am a nonsense and continue to be, still whatever I am, I have surrendered to you. Now please kindly do whatever is necessary to make me Kṛṣṇa conscious. My own struggling attempts are all useless.

I don't have much scriptural or any other knowledge, I'm not austere, I'm always losing in the struggle to control my mind, I'm insensitive to others; like this, I have so many disqualifications. Hopeless case. But (in one sense) I don't even care too much because I'm relying on your causeless mercy. I know that you are very merciful and that if I can just stick to the principle of trying to please you, then I won't need to do anything else; my whole life will be perfect. *Tomāra karuṇā—sāra:* your mercy is all that I am made of. I know that if I just stick to your lotus feet you will gradually set all my wrongs right, by your causeless mercy.

Śrīla Prabhupāda, your causeless mercy is manifested as service to you. There is no possibility for my advancement in Kṛṣṇa consciousness outside the scope of your service. Attachment to your lotus feet means service to your lotus feet. I pray to Kṛṣṇa to bless me with such attachment. Service to your lotus feet is the greatest opportunity, the greatest challenge, the source of all bliss, and the life of all your disciples. Without it, we would certainly drop back very, very deeply into material existence.

Śrīla Prabhupāda, you always stressed service. Your eternal occupation is to expand the service of the Lord by training disciples in a service attitude (Cc *Ādi* 1.44, purport). Scholars translate the word *bhakti* as "devotion," but you translated and lived it as "devotional service." What made you unique among your godbrothers was your attitude of service to your spiritual master. You only wanted to serve. You didn't want to waste even a moment. You didn't aspire for material comforts, facility, name, position, glory, or anything else. When they came as a by-product of service, you matter-of-factly accepted them, without giving them much importance. What was important to you was service to your spiritual master.

You once explained how you had wondered how it was that you, among all your godbrothers, had become successful. Several of your godbrothers were deeply learned scholars, pleasing orators, and renowned sannyasis. Unlike you, many had extensive personal association with Śrīla Bhaktisiddhānta Sarasvatī Ṭhākura. How, then, among all of them had you alone been successful? "When I analyze," you explained, "I see that of all my godbrothers only I had full faith in the order of our spiritual master." You quoted: "*Guru-mukha-padma-vākya cittete koriyā aikya, āra nā koriho mane āśā:* 'My only wish is to have my consciousness purified by the words emanating from the lotus mouth of my spiritual master.'" Thank you, Śrīla Prabhupāda, for being a real *ācārya,* not just teaching by your words but by your very life.

Let us have faith in your words, Śrīla Prabhupāda. And let us serve you single-mindedly. This is our *paramparā.* We need not waste time debating what is or is not *paramparā;* we have only to hear from and serve the *paramparā.* If we can collapse at the end of every day exhausted from a full day's service, only to get energy to serve you again—then that is causeless mercy. May our days and our lives be like that. Life without service to your lotus feet is not life at all; it is living death. If we can't serve you, then what is the use of sustaining our lives?

Śrīla Prabhupāda, you taught us guru-*bhakti.* Not a ritual, not something that had to be done just because the *śāstras* say so, not something to be legislated or speculated on, but alive, powerful. You were attached to your guru, you showered down mercy on us, and we actually loved you.

Love is a very inadequate term. That very simple, natural, and deep relationship of the soul, a spontaneous but continuous outflowing from the heart that continues to increase even in the physical absence of the object of love (in this case, yourself)—such love, though long forgotten, buried deep in our hearts, is the very essence of our existence; such love, which even in the first stage of development easily defeats the petty so-called love of this material world, even though unimaginably wonderful in the beginning, continues increasing even more unimaginably up to the point of actual love, love of Kṛṣṇa—and even then goes on increasing; such love you ignited in our hearts, then kindled with your words, activities, gestures, encouragement, and chastisement, until our hearts blazed with the desire to serve you and your beloved Kṛṣṇa.

The Kṛṣṇa consciousness movement spread all over the world because of your love. Your love was for guru and Kṛṣṇa; you desired to satisfy them in all respects. And we only desired to serve you and your Kṛṣṇa. You sacrificed everything to please your guru, and you instilled the same spirit in us; otherwise, how could the Kṛṣṇa consciousness movement spread as it did? It was materially impossible.

But you did not stick to the material. You were from the world of the unlimited. You did not think that service to guru meant giving a few lectures, initiating some widows, and indulging in theoretical conversations about advanced levels of devotion. As you wrote, "A great heritage brings responsibility in the matter of proper discharge of duties." (*Bhagavad-gītā* 2.14, purport) Being the disciple of none other than Śrī Śrīmad Bhaktisiddhānta Sarasvatī Ṭhākura, the incomparable, transcendentally mighty, sunlike effulgent *ācārya*, you always felt that you had to do the unlimited, and Kṛṣṇa responded unlimitedly. You mercifully gave unlimited souls a glimpse of the unlimited. Despite being on the platform of empowered unlimitedness, you always considered yourself a humble

servant of your spiritual master and felt keenly your bond of relationship with him. Thank you, Śrīla Prabhupāda, for being a real *ācārya,* not just teaching by words but by your very life. You are "the *ācārya* in the true sense of the term, who is authorized to deliver Kṛṣṇa." (Cc *Ādi* 1.47, purport) You are undoubtedly such a self-realized spiritual master.

Śrīla Prabhupāda, you have written in *Bhagavad-gītā As It Is:* "Satisfaction of the self-realized spiritual master is the secret of advancement in spiritual life" (4.34, purport) and "One should accept the instruction of the bona fide spiritual master as one's mission in life." (2.41, purport) When you first read these instructions in the Sanskrit *Gītā* commentary of Śrīla Viśvanātha Cakravartī Ṭhākura, they entered deep into your heart and shaped your whole life's mission. You trained your disciples like that also, so that when I was mercifully allowed to join this movement, the devotees kindly instructed me: "In everything you do, always think how to please Śrīla Prabhupāda." The whole movement was powering ahead on this simple but infallible principle.

Despite being inducted into and nurtured in such Prabhupāda consciousness, in course of time I became deluded by imaginary notions of being spiritually advanced. I gradually deteriorated into subtly looking for ways to try to enjoy Kṛṣṇa consciousness in self-centered ways. By your mercy, however, you did not reject me, and the self-introspection which followed my inevitable dissatisfaction led me once again to realize my dependence on the dust of your lotus feet.

So this is my conviction: that the only way to understand the Absolute Truth, Śrī Kṛṣṇa, is to follow you completely, without any deviation. I don't have to read a million books, grow a beard, stay up all night or artificially try to become a *gopī.* I just have to follow your simple and straightforward instructions.

That's all. It's really as easy as that. Others may say or think or do what they like (and even say, think, or do so many things in your name), but for me at least, as far as this tiny one soul is concerned, my path is very clear: follow your instructions (without introducing half-chicken logic), read your books with full faith that this is one hundred percent truth (*sarvam etad ṛtaṁ manye yan māṁ vadasi*), and pray to you continuously for guidance to follow you correctly. Step by step, I entrust my life to you, Śrīla Prabhupāda.

Śrīla Prabhupāda, I'm such a long way from Kṛṣṇa, but I know that if you are pleased with me, then, as and when you wish, you will give me Kṛṣṇa. By your causeless mercy you picked us up from *māyā*, by your causeless mercy you keep us going, and by your causeless mercy you will one day introduce us to Kṛṣṇa, face to face. *Kṛṣṇa se tomāra, kṛṣṇa dite pāro, tomāra śakati āche:* "Kṛṣṇa is yours, you have the power to give us Kṛṣṇa."

As you write (in your purport to SB 5.1.10): "By the blessings of a Vaiṣṇava, everything is possible." This statement gives me hope. Indeed, I have based my whole life on it.

You also write (in your "Prayer to the Lotus Feet of Kṛṣṇa"):

tomāra se śakti pele guru-sevāya bastu mile
jīvana sārthaka jadi hoy
sei se sevā pāile tāhale sukhī hale
tāra saṅga bhāgyate miloy

> If You bestow Your power, by serving the spiritual master one attains the Absolute Truth—one's life becomes successful. If that service is obtained, then one becomes happy and gets Your association due to good fortune.

Thus, by the mercy of Kṛṣṇa one gets guru, and by the mercy of guru one gets Kṛṣṇa. Of course, to get direct service to Kṛṣṇa is a very great and rare achievement. I don't have such a bold ambition as of now.

This is my desire, though it may be selfish: I just want to see you. Śrīla Prabhupāda, maybe it is a foolish desire. You said that personal association is for fools. Śrīla Prabhupāda, I am a fool. I want to see your lotus feet and place them on my head at least once every lifetime. I want to leave this body meditating very intensely on your lotus feet. And then, although I cannot ever deserve it, I request that I may be brought into your presence wherever you are and that you will kindly place your lotus feet on my head and cast your merciful glance upon me. This is my ambition and desire.

Śrīla Prabhupāda, I pray to you for the strength to check my madness. I don't want that when the time comes to quit this body, I will have to lament a wasted life. I cannot expect to achieve much, but I want to be able to honestly present myself to you and say, "I tried."

Śrīla Prabhupāda, you identified yourself as a soldier of Kṛṣṇa. You prayed to Kṛṣṇa for the benediction to fight for Him up to the last breath, as Arjuna did. So please induct me as a soldier in your army. Please push me into the preaching fight, despite my unwillingness—"With Prabhupāda and Kṛṣṇa on the battlefield of life."

Śrīla Prabhupāda, you have many disciples. All have their realizations of you and their relationship with you. In the future, more and more souls will come to the umbrella shade of your lotus feet. I am just one of many, many "*duḥkhīs*" who by your causeless mercy have become "*sukhī*." Śrīla Prabhupāda, please keep a place for me also in the dust of your lotus feet.

Your still fallen but ever hopeful servant,
Bhaktivikāśa Swami

1992

Dear Śrīla Prabhupāda,

Please accept my humble obeisances at your lotus feet.

nama oṁ viṣṇu-pādāya kṛṣṇa-preṣṭhāya bhū-tale
śrīmate bhaktivedānta-svāminn iti nāmine
namas te sārasvate deve gaura-vāṇī-pracāriṇe
nirviśeṣa-śūnyavādi-pāścātya-deśa-tāriṇe

This year, at Vyāsa-*pūjā*, I am offering this to you, Śrīla Prabhupāda: a section in a book I have compiled called *A Beginner's Guide to Kṛṣṇa Consciousness*. It is called:

The Importance of Śrīla Prabhupāda

The honorific title "Prabhupāda" is properly used for designating those very great spiritual masters who have made an outstanding contribution of literature and/or preaching to the world. Examples are Śrīla Rūpa Gosvāmī Prabhupāda, Śrīla Jīva Gosvāmī Prabhupāda, and Śrīla Bhaktisiddhānta Sarasvatī Gosvāmī Prabhupāda.

When members of ISKCON speak of "Śrīla Prabhupāda," they refer to His Divine Grace A.C. Bhaktivedanta Swami Prabhupāda, who is also correctly addressed as "Śrīla Prabhupāda," for he occupies a unique position in the religious history of the world.

In *Śrīmad-Bhāgavatam* (1.5.11) Śrīla Vyāsadeva states that the *Bhāgavatam* is "meant to bring about a revolution in the impious lives of this world's misdirected civilization."

Learned Vaiṣṇava scholars have discerned that this statement of Vyāsadeva's must refer to the preaching mission brought by Śrīla A.C. Bhaktivedanta Swami Prabhupāda. It was he only who, five thousand years after Śrīla Vyāsadeva's compilation of the *Bhāgavatam,* wrote his Bhaktivedanta purports on the *Bhāgavatam.* Śrīla Prabhupāda considered these purports his most important contribution for the revolutionary respiritualization of the entire human society, which had become plunged into the darkness of materialism.

Śrī Caitanya Mahāprabhu also predicted that His holy name would be broadcast in every town and village of the world. *Ācāryas* of His *sampradāya* predicted that the spread of Kṛṣṇa consciousness would usher in a Golden Age within the Age of Kali that will last fourteen thousand years. And in *Śrī Caitanya-maṅgala,* Locana Dāsa Ṭhākura predicted that a great *senāpati* (general) would appear in order to spread Lord Caitanya's message very widely. That confidential task of spreading Kṛṣṇa consciousness all over the world was entrusted to His Divine Grace A.C. Bhaktivedanta Swami Prabhupāda.

Śrī Caitanya-caritāmṛta confirms that only one who is specifically empowered by Kṛṣṇa can infuse Kṛṣṇa consciousness into the hearts of the masses.

Śrīla Bhaktivinoda Ṭhākura, a great Vaiṣṇava *ācārya* who appeared in the nineteenth century, predicted: "Very soon a great personality will appear who will spread Kṛṣṇa consciousness all over the world." That great personality is clearly His Divine Grace A.C. Bhaktivedanta Swami Prabhupāda.

Bhaktivinoda Ṭhākura also said that the greatness of a Vaiṣṇava can be understood by seeing how many nondevotees he can convert to Vaiṣṇavism. Ordinarily, to bring even a highly qualified person to Kṛṣṇa consciousness is considered a very difficult task. But Śrīla Prabhupāda was so much empowered by Kṛṣṇa that he went among the most unlikely candidates—the hedonistic youth of the Western countries—and made devotees by the thousands.

No one can fully understand the extraordinary task Śrīla Prabhupāda performed. He went alone among persons with no standard of Vedic culture. They had been brought up in a society that vigorously promoted meat-eating, illicit sex, gambling, and intoxication. They had no idea of how to receive a sadhu. They were in almost every way totally disqualified as candidates for spiritual life.

Śrīla Prabhupāda not only went among such people, but he gradually managed to train many of them to such an extent that they are now accepted everywhere as first-class Vaiṣṇavas and preachers, qualified to impart Kṛṣṇa consciousness to others.

There were certainly many Vaiṣṇavas in India who were devoted, learned, and renowned. However, the fact remains that it was Śrīla Prabhupāda alone who was sufficiently qualified to spread Kṛṣṇa consciousness all over the world. Only he had sufficient faith in the instructions of Lord Caitanya, the order of his spiritual master, and the holy name of Kṛṣṇa to seriously attempt spreading Kṛṣṇa consciousness outside India. Only he had that much compassion and vision to preach the message of Lord Caitanya to those who most needed it. Only one of the topmost confidential devotees of Kṛṣṇa could perform such an extraordinary task. His unparalleled achievements make it clear that he occupies a unique position in the history of Vaiṣṇavism.

Śrīla Prabhupāda was empowered to spread Kṛṣṇa consciousness in a very practical and straightforward way, just suitable for the modern world. Without changing or compromising the teachings of Kṛṣṇa consciousness even slightly, he presented its esoteric truths in a clear and intelligible manner, suitable for both the scholar and the layman simultaneously.

Śrīla Prabhupāda personally oversaw the expansion and development of ISKCON. He set up the programs that were to form the basis of ISKCON's continued expansion: production and distribution of transcendental literature, *harināma-saṅkīrtana* parties, temples and *āśramas*, *prasāda* distribution, transcendental farm communities, *gurukulas*, preaching to scientists and intellectuals, etc. Śrīla Prabhupāda personally gave detailed directions in every aspect of Kṛṣṇa consciousness: how to worship the Deities, how to conduct *sādhana*, how to preach, how to wear a *dhotī*, how to cook for Kṛṣṇa, how to chant mantras, and so on.

Śrīla Prabhupāda is thus the founder-*ācārya* of ISKCON. Whatever standards and instructions we have in ISKCON come from him. Thus Śrīla Prabhupāda will always remain the main *śikṣā*-guru for all members of ISKCON.

Both scripture and tradition offer various approaches to Kṛṣṇa consciousness. But followers of Śrīla Prabhupāda execute Kṛṣṇa consciousness just as he showed them. They know that Śrīla Prabhupāda, as a faithful follower of his guru and the previous *ācāryas*, presented Kṛṣṇa consciousness in the best way for the modern age. Śrīla Prabhupāda's success is itself proof that his endeavors are approved, ordained, and blessed by the Supreme Lord Śrī Kṛṣṇa Himself. Śrīla Prabhupāda gave certain instructions that are absolutely necessary for initiated disciples to follow if they at all want to claim to be serious devotees or genuine followers of Śrīla Prabhupāda. For instance: Śrīla Prabhupāda demanded that initiated devotees rise by 4:00 a.m., attend *maṅgala-ārati*, chant a minimum of sixteen rounds of the *mahā-mantra* every day, and scrupulously follow the four regulative principles.

All such standards that Śrīla Prabhupāda clearly defined are standards to be followed in ISKCON. A rightly situated, successful follower of Śrīla Prabhupāda is simply a faithful standard-bearer. He does not try to change or interpret the standards and programs given by Śrīla Prabhupāda, for he knows that what Śrīla Prabhupāda has given us is perfectly complete and completely perfect for the respiritualization of the entire human society—not only now, but for the next ten thousand years.

Śrīla Prabhupāda, please accept my clumsy efforts to glorify you. Please empower us all to glorify you more by widely spreading knowledge of your greatness, along with that of your beloved Lord Kṛṣṇa. Please bless us all to never lose sight of your wonderful lotus feet. Please forgive me for still making so many offenses in my bumbling efforts to please you. Most of all, I beg you, shouting desperately, that however much of a nonsense rascal I am, please never let me go.

Offered by this nasty pinprick in the dust of your lotus feet,

Ever desiring your mercy,

Your eternal servant,
Bhaktivikāśa Swami

1993

The 1992 Vyāsa-*pūjā* book seems to be the best yet. Many of the offerings of the senior devotees express deep, mature realizations. Most hearteningly, the understanding of Śrīla Prabhupāda's pre-eminent position in ISKCON, his incomparable status, and of our smallness before him, seems to be widespread even amongst the initiating gurus of ISKCON today. Many great souls are traveling here and there, carrying the flag of Kṛṣṇa, repeating Kṛṣṇa's words as received through Śrīla Prabhupāda, and thus purifying the world (*vaiṣṇavāḥ kṣiti-pāvanāḥ*). With this encouragement, I sit to write my Vyāsa-*pūjā* offering for 1993.

nama oṁ viṣṇu-pādāya kṛṣṇa-preṣṭhāya bhū-tale
śrīmate bhaktivedānta-svāminn iti nāmine
namas te sārasvate deve gaura-vāṇī-pracāriṇe
nirviśeṣa-śūnyavādi-pāścātya-deśa-tāriṇe

Dear Śrīla Prabhupāda,

Please accept my humble obeisances. All glories to your lotus feet.

As the people of the world prepare to burn, bomb, and bludgeon each other into nonexistence, the inevitable finale of a mad atheistic civilization that tried to replace God with machines; as the secular liberals and pseudo-intellectuals raise their hands in useless horror, crying, "Oh no, oh no"; the Vaiṣṇavas still try to spread your message.

Will the world listen? Maybe a few. But it may be too little, and too late. If only they would listen to you, Śrīla Prabhupāda!

You gave everything. How to live peacefully, accepting nature's gifts, relying on Kṛṣṇa and making Him the goal of life. But they took you as "another swami," someone to maybe show a little curious respect to but certainly not to be taken very seriously.

You warned them, but they did not care to hear. The karmic fruits have become so heavy that we can hardly imagine what horrors lie ahead.

And after that? Will the survivors again pay lip-service to God and slip back into Māyāvāda, deftly avoiding Kṛṣṇa?

Or will they at last accept you as the real teacher, the one who gave all the answers, the world savior who brought the light of the *Bhāgavata* to guide us for the next ten thousand years?

That depends a lot on us. Will we recognize your pre-eminent glories as the greatest devotee in the modern age? Will we glorify you throughout the universe? Or will we also not listen to you? Will we say, "Maybe Śrīla Prabhupāda didn't mean this, he meant that?" Will we also avoid you, mix up your teachings with those of less realized sadhus, rationalize you, and marginalize you?

Śrīla Prabhupāda, your glories shine like the sun. Those who are honest cannot but be overwhelmed at the tremendous, incomparable good you have done to human society by giving us Kṛṣṇa as He is. The owls close their eyes in the day and "wisely" elaborate on the nonexistence or only relative importance of the sun. Śrīla Prabhupāda, I am a rascal. You know that. But I pray from you the blessing that I never be such a rascal as to leave your lotus feet or think the shade of your lotus feet to be only a relative factor in my spiritual advancement. I also pray for the blessing to be always aware of my duty to you to try to spread the message of Kṛṣṇa as you spoke it, confident in the hope that sanity will some time prevail, and that the world will recognize who you are and finally start to listen to you.

Please give me the benediction of becoming an effective preacher of the Vaiṣṇava cult. I know that this is no small thing to ask! Inspired, effective preaching requires purity, realization, and compassion. The world needs hundreds and thousands of preachers. Therefore you requested all your disciples to become preachers. You will be happy to award such a benediction if we are actually sincere to receive it. I especially ask to become an instrument in the *pāṣaṇḍa-dalana* department—helping to fulfil your ambition of driving atheism out of the world by establishing Kṛṣṇa consciousness as it is: *sarva-dharmān parityajya mām ekaṁ śaraṇaṁ vraja.*

Even more specifically, I seek your blessings to write for Kṛṣṇa. Kṛṣṇa inspires different devotees to serve His mission in different ways. It may be presumptuous, but I feel strongly the urge to write. It is not easy to write properly for Kṛṣṇa. Writing is fighting. Strong, clear expression is required. False egoism or speculation will defeat our purpose and publicly declare our foolishness. My writing should be to lead others to the path you have shown us. My egoism should not stand between the reader and your message. Transparency and purity are needed. That is difficult to attain. Therefore I request you to kindly infuse your spirit in every letter I write. I should not write to please scholars or sycophant-collectors, but to please you. Without your blessings, my writing will be devoid of potency, and therefore useless. Please bless me to always remember this. Please bless me also that my writing not be too much inhibited by the headaches that have disturbed me for the last few years.

Dear Śrīla Prabhupāda, please bless me to always do what is pleasing you. This may sound like a very straightforward and ordinary request, but these days even senior devotees who had much association with you, and have stayed in your movement all these years, have different opinions over what or what not to do. To bust ghosts, or not? Whether or not to directly attempt for elevated, intimate levels of devotion. What is the origin of the *jīva*, anyway? These are important questions that in your personal presence would be resolved with just a few words from your lotus mouth. Now we are not sure—or rather, we have different parties all sure differently. What we can be sure of is that you wanted preaching, book distribution, *harināma* in every town and village, Kṛṣṇa recognized as the Supreme Personality of Godhead, and atheism smashed. We can also be sure that if we dedicate these short lives to pleasing you by these activities, you will be kind upon us. Our first, main, and only business is to please you. No one (hardly anyone in ISKCON, anyway) disputes that. But sometimes there are transcendental (hopefully) differences over how to please you.

Even in your manifest presence, devotees would sometimes do something they thought would please you but that instead incurred your wrath. Learning to please the self-realized spiritual master is the essence of spiritual life, but it may not always be so easy, especially in his physical absence. So please guide us that we may be intelligent enough (not overintelligent!) to serve you exactly as you desire.

Śrīla Prabhupāda, please bless us that our hearts may be soft and loving. Isn't that what Kṛṣṇa consciousness is all about, anyway? Often, in the hurly-burly of ISKCON life, we forget who our friends are and become inconsiderate, unkind, and hard-hearted. For all our advancement, seniority, and respectability, we seem to be far from the simple, open-hearted dealings that so attracted us when we first joined. Of course, simply mouthing a prayer, or even getting it printed in the Vyāsa-*pūjā* book, will not change much. We have to work on cleaning our hearts and examining our motives. Please bestow your mercy that we may construct your house so that the whole world will be welcome and happy to live in it. Developments only of bricks and stone will not serve your purpose.

Śrīla Prabhupāda, please bless me with pure devotion at the lotus feet of your beloved Lord Kṛṣṇa. Please bless me with a taste for hearing and chanting the holy names. Please bless me that my heart be free of envy and lust.

Vyāsa-*pūjā* offerings are meant principally for glorification, not so much for begging boons. Rightly or wrongly, I have made many requests from you in this offering. You once said in a conversation (September 12, 1973) that your blessings are already there, we just have to take them and fight. Your blessings are there, but unless we remember that everything is going on by their power, we will lose them and thus lose everything. Therefore, as a young child is always anxious not to lose sight of his mother, I am asking never to lose sight of you. My final request this year is that I always remain as if a child protected by your lotus feet, and that I always act as a responsible son to help preserve the legacy of the father.

Your rotten servant,
Bhakti Vikāsa Swami*

1994

Dear Śrīla Prabhupāda,

Please accept my humble obeisances at your divine lotus feet.

nama oṁ viṣṇu-pādāya kṛṣṇa-preṣṭhāya bhū-tale
śrīmate bhaktivedānta-svāminn iti nāmine
namas te sārasvate deve gaura-vāṇī-pracāriṇe
nirviśeṣa-śūnyavādi-pāścātya-deśa-tāriṇe

Śrīla Prabhupāda, in my last Vyāsa-*pūjā* offering (which unfortunately was not published in the 1993 Vyāsa-*pūjā* book, for what reason I do not know) I asked for the benediction to be able to engage in writing as my service. By your grace, the two major obstacles hindering my writing have been removed, at least temporarily. By your grace, I have been able to offer you three new books in the last year, namely *A Message to the Youth of India*, *Vaṁśīdāsa Bābājī*, and *Jaya Śrīla Prabhupāda*! (the last is a special offering to your Divine Grace). I have also been able to bring out some of my books in different languages. By your

* Submitted for inclusion but not featured in the Vyāsa-*pūjā* book of 1993.

grace also, my writings have been well received. I feel very happy to be able to contribute in this small way to the furtherance of your mission. I thank you for allowing me to serve in this way, and request your continued blessings to go on with this work.

Here are some observations about your mission that I am submitting to you as my 1994 Vyāsa-*pūjā* offering.

Śrīla Prabhupāda established Kṛṣṇa consciousness in the Western world and planted the seeds for a great spiritual upsurge. He emphasized the distribution of his books as the best means to bring about a revolution in the misdirected lives of a godless civilization.

Since the departure of Śrīla Prabhupāda in 1977, his movement has been through many ups and downs. However, the book distribution and preaching has always continued. Sadly, in strategically important America, book distribution has greatly declined. However, the many millions of books that have been distributed there in the past are having their effect.

Śrīla Prabhupāda predicted that his books would change the world and perceived their effect in all spheres of life. For instance, when Śrīla Prabhupāda was informed that a major platform of Jimmy Carter's successful Presidential campaign was his commitment to religion, Prabhupāda ascribed the prominence being given to religion as a result of his preaching.

Today, despite the continued ravages of Kali-yuga, there are similar encouraging signs. For instance, twenty years ago in the West, vegetarianism was looked upon as a crazy fad. Now it is an accepted lifestyle for millions. Similarly, many have foregone alcohol and tobacco. The external cause for these major behavioral changes is health considerations. However, devotees recognize the underlying influence of the mode of goodness brought about by the distribution of Śrīla Prabhupāda's books.

Even more excitingly, the truths of karma and reincarnation are becoming ever more widely accepted in the West. At least there is a widespread awareness of the concept of reincarnation. Twenty years ago there was not.

Another positive development is "Straight Edge." Thousands of young Americans now eschew, or aspire to eschew, nonvegetarian food, intoxication, gambling and (amazingly!) illicit sex. Better still, they are spiritual seekers, and are open to Kṛṣṇa. Their numbers may not be significant, but their ideals are.

Perhaps the most important development, however, is in the field of science—that most conservative bastion of sophisticated godlessness. Śrīla Prabhupāda saw materialistic scientists as high priests of a society deliberately turned away from God. Prabhupāda was certain that if the attention of scientists could somehow be focused on *bhagavat-tattva-vijñāna,* they would gradually have to acknowledge its superiority. Convincing scientists is practically our most important preaching, for if they accept Kṛṣṇa consciousness, everyone else will follow. Winning over scientists is not easy, and overnight changes are not to be expected. However, there are very encouraging signs.

Consider the following extract from "Cosmos, Bios, Theos," a 1992 survey of the views of seventy top scientists:

> Stranger than the strangest concepts and theories of science is the appearance of God on the intellectual horizon of late twentieth-century science. Pioneers and giants of modern science like Einstein, Planck, and Heisenberg were equally at home with the "hard facts" of science and with a theological frame of reference. The paradox persists to this very day. Einstein once said "I want to know how God created this world.... I want to know His thoughts, the rest are details." Stephen Hawking, the theoretical physicist who is often

> described as Einstein's successor, has declared in his recent best seller, *A Brief History of Time*, that our goal should be to "know the mind of God." And astrophysicist Robert Jastrow begins *God and the Astronomers*, his celebrated survey of modern cosmology, with a remarkable observation: "For the scientist who has lived by his faith in the power of reason, the story ends like a bad dream. He has scaled the mountain of ignorance; he is about to conquer the highest peak; as he pulls himself over the final rock, he is greeted by a band of theologians who have been sitting there for centuries."

Previously, scientists rejected Biblical concepts of creation and cosmology as being grossly inaccurate and superstitious. Today, the scientist, in his quest for ever deeper knowledge of the universe, finds himself back at the door of transcendence. The modern philosopher of science, in his metaphysical wanderings, is not restricted to Christian theology, for present day seekers of truth are free to avail of the many systems of religion and philosophy extant in the world. Recent attempts to wed science with the supramundane mostly led to the "Tao of Physics" type of impersonalistic speculation. It is significant to note from such publications as "Cosmos, Bios, Theos," that several highly reputed scientists are now gravitating towards the understanding of God as the supreme controller of the laws of nature. In his books, Śrīla Prabhupāda presents knowledge of God and His energies with a clarity and depth not available from any other source. Therefore, it is quite feasible that in the not too distant future, *bhagavat-tattva-vijñāna*, the *Bhāgavata* philosophy in Śrīla Prabhupāda's books will become accepted in scientific circles, first, as a legitimate hypothesis of reality, and eventually as the guiding light for major breakthroughs in scientific understanding.

Apart from these subtle but significant developments in human thought and behavior, the overt influence of the Hare Kṛṣṇa movement is worth examining.

The astonishing rapid growth of Kṛṣṇa consciousness in the ex-communist bloc continues unabated. These tremendous advances in a large and significant area of the planet promise to be a prominent factor in establishing Kṛṣṇa consciousness as a major world religious force.

In the West also, there are good signs. The movement is well established having been around for almost thirty years. Many people like devotees, think of them as good people, and appreciate their dedication, joyful chanting, and *prasāda* distribution. Many young people, especially, think of the Hare Kṛṣṇas as being a genuinely spiritual movement.

In India, ISKCON has become a household word. ISKCON is widely respected for its worldwide propagation of Kṛṣṇa-*bhakti*, its exemplary standard of Deity worship, and for the sincerity, purity and strictness of its members. Whereas, twenty years ago, devotees often met with the response, "I am a Hindu and I know everything," it is now not unusual for highly-educated and well-positioned Indians to approach Western devotees and respectfully submit, "We Hindus now have to learn about our own culture and religion from you."

In India, where impersonalism ruled supreme for so long, the power of Śrīla Prabhupāda's books is beginning to manifest. Many Hindus are now emerging from the confusion of Māyāvāda to understand *Bhagavad-gītā As It Is*—unconditional surrender to Lord Śrī Kṛṣṇa, the Supreme Personality of Godhead.

In all ways, on all fronts, the preaching field is opening up and getting more and more exciting. This is all the grace of Lord Caitanya, as manifest through the activities of his most dear devotee, His Divine Grace A.C. Bhaktivedanta Swami Prabhupāda. There is tremendous scope for our movement to surge forward and do truly amazing things.

Perhaps our best offering to Śrīla Prabhupāda for his Centennial celebration would be to offer ourselves, the members of his movement, as a truly united family, serving together with full trust and cooperation, combinedly working towards the goal that Śrīla Prabhupāda wanted most of all—a new world order under the flag of Kṛṣṇa.

All glories to your lotus feet, Śrīla Prabhupāda.

Your most insignificant servant,
Bhakti Vikāsa Swami

1995

nama oṁ viṣṇu-pādāya kṛṣṇa-preṣṭhāya bhū-tale
śrīmate bhaktivedānta-svāminn iti nāmine
namas te sārasvate deve gaura-vāṇī-pracāriṇe
nirviśeṣa-śūnyavādi-pāścātya-deśa-tāriṇe

Śrīla Prabhupāda was always writing, speaking, and singing about Kṛṣṇa, remaining absorbed in His service in full ecstasy and realization. By his mercy, we also write, speak, and sing for Kṛṣṇa and engage in His and Prabhupāda's service. On his order, we "do as he did." But our writing, singing, and serving cannot compare to his, for Prabhupāda's purity and realization far surpass our own.

Therefore for this year's Vyāsa-*pūjā* I am offering a collection of Prabhupāda's writings and sayings. Although Śrīla Prabhupāda spoke on a wide variety of subjects, all connected to Kṛṣṇa and Kṛṣṇa consciousness, I have chosen a topic particularly relevant at the present time: Śrīla Prabhupāda's explanation of his own unique position.

Śrīla Prabhupāda was the ideal of a pure devotee. Although his achievements in Kṛṣṇa's service were unprecedented and inimitable, he remained humble and gave the credit to his spiritual master. Still, considering our rascal tendency to be misled by bluffers and cheaters, Śrīla Prabhupāda sometimes delineated his actual position: that he is the special representative of Lord Caitanya, a *śaktyāveśa-avatāra,* and the only true disciple of his guru. Just as Lord Caitanya sometimes behaved like a common man and sometimes manifested His Godly opulence (cf. Cc *Antya* 8.93), so similarly Śrīla Prabhupāda sometimes clearly let us know that he was a special devotee sent by Lord Caitanya to spread His name all over the world.

As Śrīla Prabhupāda explains in his purport to *Caitanya-caritāmṛta Madhya* 25.9, quoted below, by sincere study and appreciation of the personal characteristics of devotees we can understand who is actually authorized and especially empowered.

As Gaṅgā is offered to Gaṅgā, I offer the following quotes for the pleasure of Śrīla Prabhupāda and the enlightenment of his followers.

> If one saw the personal characteristics and activities of Śrī Caitanya Mahāprabhu, one would certainly be convinced that He was the Supreme Personality of Godhead. One can ascertain this by following in the footsteps of the śāstric injunctions. This sincere study and appreciation of Śrī Caitanya Mahāprabhu is also applicable to His authorized devotees, and it is clearly stated in the *Caitanya-caritāmṛta* (*Antya-līlā,* 7.11):
>
> *kali-kālera dharma—kṛṣṇa-nāma-saṅkīrtana*
> *kṛṣṇa-śakti vinā nāhe tāra pravartana*
>
> In this Age of Kali, real religious propaganda should induce people to chant the Hare Kṛṣṇa *mahā-mantra.* This is possible

for someone who is especially empowered by Kṛṣṇa. No one can do this without being especially favored by Kṛṣṇa.

Śrīla Bhaktisiddhānta Sarasvatī Ṭhākura comments in this regard in his *Anubhāṣya,* wherein he quotes a verse from *Nārāyaṇa-saṁhitā: dvāparīyair janair viṣṇuḥ pañcarātrais tu kevalaiḥ/ kalau tu nāma-mātreṇa pūjyate bhagavān hariḥ.*

"In Dvāpara-yuga, devotees of Lord Viṣṇu and Kṛṣṇa rendered devotional service according to the principles of *Pañcarātra.* In this Age of Kali, the Supreme Personality of Godhead is worshipped simply by the chanting of His names." Śrīla Bhaktisiddhānta Sarasvatī Ṭhākura then comments, 'Without being empowered by the direct potency of Lord Kṛṣṇa to fulfil His desire and without being specifically favored by the Lord, no human being can become the spiritual master of the whole world. He certainly cannot succeed by mental concoction, which is not meant for devotees or religious people. Only an empowered personality can distribute the holy name of the Lord and enjoin all fallen souls to worship Kṛṣṇa. By distributing the holy name of the Lord, he cleanses the hearts of the most fallen people; therefore he extinguishes the blazing fire of the material world. Not only that, he broadcasts the shining brightness of Kṛṣṇa's effulgence throughout the world. Such an *ācārya,* or spiritual master, should be considered nondifferent from Kṛṣṇa—that is, he should be considered the incarnation of Lord Kṛṣṇa's potency. Such a personality is *kṛṣṇāliṅgita-vigraha*—that is, he is always embraced by the Supreme Personality of Godhead, Kṛṣṇa. Such a person is above the considerations of the *varṇāśrama* institution. He is the guru or spiritual master for the entire world, a devotee on the topmost platform, the *mahā-bhāgavata* stage, and a *paramahaṁsa-ṭhākura,* a spiritual form only fit to be addressed as *paramahaṁsa* or *ṭhākura.*"

Nonetheless, there are many people who are just like owls but never open their eyes to see the sunshine. These owlish personalities are inferior to the Māyāvādī *sannyāsīs* who

cannot see the brilliance of Kṛṣṇa's favor upon the *mahā-bhāgavata* devotee. They are prepared to criticize the person engaged in distributing the holy name all over the world and following in the footsteps of Śrī Caitanya Mahāprabhu, who wanted Kṛṣṇa consciousness preached in every town and city. (Cc *Madhya* 25.9, purport)

When King Pṛthu is described as an incarnation of Lord Viṣṇu, it should be understood that he is a *śaktyāveśa-avatāra,* part and parcel of Lord Viṣṇu, and is specifically empowered by Him. Any living being acting as the incarnation of Lord Viṣṇu is thus empowered by Lord Viṣṇu to preach the *bhakti* cult. Such a person can act like Lord Viṣṇu and defeat demons by arguments and preach the *bhakti* cult exactly according to the principles of *śāstra.* As indicated in *Bhagavad-gītā,* whenever we find someone extraordinary preaching the *bhakti* cult, we should know that he is especially empowered by Lord Viṣṇu, or Lord Kṛṣṇa. As confirmed in *Caitanya-caritāmṛta* (*Antya* 7.11), *kṛṣṇa-śakti vinā nahe tāra pravartana:* one cannot explain the glories of the holy name of the Lord without being specifically empowered by Him. If one criticizes or finds fault with such an empowered personality, one is to be considered an offender against Lord Viṣṇu and is punishable. Even though such offenders may dress as Vaiṣṇavas with false *tilaka* and *mālā,* they are never forgiven by the Lord if they offend a pure Vaiṣṇava. There are many instances of this in the *śāstras.* (SB 4.19.37)

A devotee, by his personal devotional service, can influence all the people of the whole world to become devotees of the Lord. If there is only one pure devotee in pure Kṛṣṇa consciousness, he can change the total consciousness of the world into Kṛṣṇa consciousness. (SB 4.8.80, purport)

Just as Kṛṣṇa does not take a step away from Vṛndāvana, Kṛṣṇa's devotee also does not like to leave Vṛndāvana. However, when he has to tend to Kṛṣṇa's business, he leaves Vṛndāvana. After finishing his mission, a pure devotee returns home, back to Vṛndāvana, back to Godhead. (Cc *Madhya* 13.156, purport)

When a Vaiṣṇava comes, when God Himself comes, or when God's sons or His very confidential devotees come, their only mission is to save sinful men who are suffering. They have knowledge of how to do this. (*Science of Self-Realization*, p. 7)

Translation:

O my worshipable Lord, because the seed of lusty desires, which is the root cause of material existence, is within the core of everyone's heart, You have sent me to this material world to exhibit the symptoms of a pure devotee.

Purport:

The *Bhakti-rasāmṛta-sindhu* has given considerable discussion about *nitya-siddha* and *sādhana-siddha* devotees. *Nitya-siddha* devotees come from Vaikuṇṭha to this material world to teach, by their personal example, how to become a devotee. The living entities in this material world can take lessons from such *nitya-siddha* devotees and thus become inclined to return home, back to Godhead. A *nitya-siddha* devotee comes from Vaikuṇṭha upon the order of the Supreme Personality of Godhead and shows by his example how to become a pure devotee (*anyābhilāṣitā-śūnyam*). In spite of coming to this material world, the *nitya-siddha* devotee is never attracted by the allurements of material enjoyment. A perfect example is Prahlāda Mahārāja, who was a *nitya-siddha*, a *mahā-bhāgavata* devotee. Although Prahlāda was born in the family of Hiraṇyakaśipu, an atheist, he was never attached to any kind of materialistic enjoyment. Desiring to exhibit the symptoms of a pure devotee, the Lord tried to induce Prahlāda Mahārāja to take material benedictions, but Prahlāda Mahārāja did not accept them. On the contrary, by his personal example he showed the symptoms of a pure devotee. In other words, the Lord Himself has no desire to send His pure devotee to this material world, nor does a devotee have any material purpose in coming. When the Lord Himself appears as an incarnation within this material world, He is not allured by the material atmosphere, and He has nothing to do with material activity, yet by His example He teaches the common man how to become a devotee. Similarly, a devotee who comes here in accordance with the order of the Supreme Lord shows by his personal behavior how to become a pure devotee. A pure devotee, therefore, is a practical example for all living entities, including Lord Brahmā. (SB 7.10.3, purport)

Just as a condemned person can be relieved by a special favor of the chief executive head, the president or king, so the condemned people of this Kali-yuga can be delivered only by the Supreme Personality of Godhead Himself or a person especially empowered for this purpose. (Cc *Ādi* 13.69, purport)

Sometimes the Lord, as the child of mother Yaśodā, requests His devotee for some food, as if He were very hungry. Sometimes He tells His devotee in a dream that His temple and His garden are now very old and that He cannot enjoy them very nicely. Thus He requests the devotee to repair them. Sometimes He is buried in the earth, and as if unable to come out Himself, He requests His devotee to rescue Him. Sometimes He requests His devotee to preach His glories all over the world, although He alone is quite competent to perform this task. Even though the Supreme Personality of Godhead is endowed with all possessions and is self-sufficient, He depends on His devotees. Therefore the relationship of the Lord with His devotees is extremely confidential. Only the devotee can perceive how the Lord, although full in Himself, depends on His devotee for some particular work. This is explained in *Bhagavad-gītā* (11.33), where the Lord tells Arjuna, *nimitta-mātraṁ bhava savyasācin*: "O Arjuna, merely be an instrument in the fight." Lord Kṛṣṇa had the competence to win the Battle of Kurukṣetra, but nonetheless He induced His devotee Arjuna to fight and become the cause of victory. Śrī Caitanya Mahāprabhu was quite competent enough to spread His name and mission all over the world, but still He depended upon His devotee to do this work. (SB 6.19.5, purport)

Let us always remember that ISKCON is not just another movement. It is Śrīla Prabhupāda and Śrīla Bhaktisiddhānta Sarasvatī Ṭhākura Prabhupāda's movement, meant for fulfilling Lord Caitanya's inner desire to save the world. As Śrīla Prabhupāda writes in his concluding words to his *Caitanya-caritāmṛta* commentary: "This Kṛṣṇa consciousness movement has been started to fulfil the desire of Śrīla Bhaktisiddhānta Sarasvatī Prabhupāda." Because Śrīla Prabhupāda had cent percent faith in the words of his spiritual master, he was uniquely successful in spreading Kṛṣṇa consciousness all over the world. If we have similar faith in Śrīla Prabhupāda's words and try to follow the unequaled and unsurpassed example he set of tirelessly working to propagate Śrī Caitanya Mahāprabhu's *saṅkīrtana* movement, we shall achieve all success in our own spiritual endeavors and properly serve our glorious founder-*ācārya*.

Submitted by the worst of your disciples,

Bhakti Vikāsa Swami

1996

Dear Śrīla Prabhupāda,

nama oṁ viṣṇu-pādāya kṛṣṇa-preṣṭhāya bhū-tale
śrīmate bhaktivedānta-svāminn iti nāmine
namas te sārasvate deve gaura-vāṇī-pracāriṇe
nirviśeṣa-śūnyavādi-pāścātya-deśa-tāriṇe

Śrīla Prabhupāda, you wanted your sannyasis to do big things—

"Make more disciples than me.

Write more books than me.

Open more temples than me."

To fulfil even one of these dictums seems for me almost impossible, but the challenge is relishable. I don't want to do anything cheaply, in an imitative way, but I do want to please you.

The preaching field is open. There are hundreds and thousands of towns and villages throughout the world, and Lord Caitanya wants His name chanted in every one of them. Millions of people are eager to know about Kṛṣṇa, only they don't know yet. They have still to be woken up by your *saṅkīrtana* soldiers, who go to every human habitation on the planet bringing your books, your message, your mercy.

You said people would come to us in the millions. They will have to be trained, protected, guided, and nourished. You have given us many lifetimes of work, but time is short and our strength limited.

Therefore, on this most auspicious occasion of your Centennial Vyāsa-*pūjā*, I am falling at your lotus feet and begging for the mercy to dive deeply into the ocean of preaching ecstasy. May my efforts to serve you expand geometrically every year. Let me do something significant in your great mission of spreading Kṛṣṇa consciousness to every home and every heart.

ekākī āmāra, nāhi pāya bala
hari-nāma-saṅkīrtane
tumi kṛpā kari', śraddhā bindu diyā
deha kṛṣṇa-nāma dhane

I do not find the strength to carry on alone the *saṅkīrtana* of the holy name of Hari. Please bless me by giving me just one

SNA

drop of faith with which to obtain the great treasure of the holy name of Kṛṣṇa.

Your eternal servant,
Bhakti-vikāsa Swami

1997

Prabhupāda Gems

nama oṁ viṣṇu-pādāya kṛṣṇa-preṣṭhāya bhū-tale
śrīmate bhaktivedānta-svāminn iti nāmine
namas te sārasvate deve gaura-vāṇī-pracāriṇe
nirviśeṣa-śūnyavādi-pāścātya-deśa-tāriṇe

Śrīla Prabhupāda, as the ideal guru you were always giving knowledge to human society. Tirelessly writing and speaking, you gave all kinds of valuable instructions, phenomenal and numinous: economic, political, psychological, medical, scientific, and of course spiritual. All *siddhāntas,* all *tattvas,* everything is there complete for redirecting human society back to the lotus feet of Kṛṣṇa. Apart from your formally written books, we also have books of your conversations, letters, and lectures. Plus, many devotees are writing their remembrances of you. All of this is like a huge mine of nectar, where any number of devotional scholars can go and happily extract valuable gems.

Personally, I take great pleasure in again and again reading your books and again and again speaking their message to others. I have also set myself at least one lifetime's work of writing books based on your books, endeavoring to give guidance on particular topics in a systematic way. As I go on mining the nectar from your books, I marvel at your dedication, ever-correctness, cutting analysis, and "as it is" kick-in-the-face frankness.

By enlightening me with knowledge, you gave me a reason to live. Even now, you continue to save me by speaking to me from your books. Your words scythe my mind and keep my Kṛṣṇa consciousness alive. As I read on and on, my gratitude to you is ever increasing. Another marvel is your allowing me to take part in the great global mission of giving these gems to others. Like a greedy man, I go on extracting gems to add to my already voluminous collection. But I am not like a miser, for there is no pleasure in that. I am more like a research student eager to share his valuable discoveries with others. One way I assist in spreading your message is by writing books based on your directions and decorated with gems from your teachings.

Śrīla Prabhupāda, your books are complete and perfect, and are available to all. Nevertheless, you instructed your disciples, especially the *sannyāsīs,* to write. "My disciples will write purports to my books." Undoubtedly, our writings must be based on yours, Śrīla Prabhupāda, or they will have no potency, meaning, or value. What else do we know, anyway?

At the very least, our writings will be for self-purification. And, if you so want to use your disciples, their books may also be valuable guides to human society.

As all I have is what you have given me, here are a few gems, offered respectfully back to you, to be shared with your ever-increasing family of appreciative devotees.

> Kṛṣṇa also becomes very beautiful. He's already beautiful. But when a devotee serves Him, a devotee comes to Him, He also becomes very beautiful. A devotee, when with his heart and soul, serves Kṛṣṇa in dressing Him, in feeding Him, in giving Him flower, He becomes smiling. And if you can get Kṛṣṇa once smiling upon you, your life is fulfilled. (Lecture on SB 3.25.12, Bombay, 12 November 1974)

Modern civilization is centered around animal-killing. *Karmīs* are advertising that without eating meat, their vitamin value or vitality will be reduced; so to keep oneself fit to work hard, one must eat meat, and to digest meat, one must drink liquor, and to keep the balance of drinking wine and eating meat, one must have sufficient sexual intercourse to keep fit to work very hard like an ass. (SB 4.27.11, purport)

There is no difficulty in coming in contact with the Supreme Lord (*ko 'ti-prayāsaḥ*). On the other hand, going to hell requires great endeavor. If one wants to go to hell by illicit sex, meat-eating, gambling, and intoxication, he must acquire so many things. For illicit sex he must arrange for money for brothels, for meat-eating he must arrange for many slaughterhouses, for gambling he must arrange for casinos and hotels, and for intoxication he must open many breweries. Clearly, therefore, if one wants to go to hell he must endeavor very much. But if he wants to return home, back to Godhead, there is no difficult endeavor. To go back to Godhead, one may live alone anywhere, in any condition, and simply sit down, meditate upon the Supersoul and chant and hear about the Lord. Thus there is no difficulty in approaching the Lord. *Adānta-gobhir viśatāṁ tamisram.* Because of inability to control the senses, one must go through great endeavor to go to hell, but if one is sensible he can very easily obtain the favor of the Supreme Personality of Godhead because the Lord is always with him. (SB 7.7.38, purport)

"You are OK. I am OK." Our proposal is not that. Our proposal is: "You are not OK. I am OK." (Lecture on SB 6.1.9, Los Angeles, 22 June 1975)

They will never surrender. This is the sign of demon. They will never surrender. They will be killed, they will go to hell, they will accept all the thing, but still, if you ask him that "You surrender to..." "No." That is demonic. (Lecture on SB 1.5.8, New Vrindaban, 24 May 1969)

So you have taken to the vow of Kṛṣṇa consciousness. Try to preach Kṛṣṇa consciousness all over the world. And we have got little success. One politician in U.S.A., he has remarked that "This Kṛṣṇa consciousness movement is increasing like an epidemic." He has said that. "And if we do not check it, one day it may take our government." He has opined like that. So any intelligent man can know what is the ultimate result. Because mass of people, if they take to Kṛṣṇa consciousness, then government is yours. That is a fact. And if the Kṛṣṇa consciousness government is there, no meat-eating, no smoking, no illicit sex, so many no's, the demons will die. (Lecture on SB 1.7.47, Vṛndāvana, 6 October 1976)

Some rascals put forward the theory that an animal has no soul or is something like dead stone. In this way they rationalize that there is no sin in animal-killing. Actually animals are not dead stone, but the killers of animals are stonehearted. Consequently no reason or philosophy appeals to them. (SB 4.26.9, purport)

Guest: I have noticed when everybody touches their head to the floor. And this I find so disturbing [indistinct] ... another man and kiss their boots. I found that [indistinct]. And to tell you frankly, I find it quite shocking, too, that people place their head on the ground before another man. And you are a man like that. You are a man of knowledge, and you're [indistinct]. But yet I can't see of people their heads to the floor.

Prabhupāda: You have been asked to do that?

Guest: Nobody asked me, but I see everybody else does it.

Prabhupāda: Then why you are feeling so disturbed?

Guest: Because to me, people are people, and there's... No man is a God, and it's just appearing as if you were...

Prabhupāda: But as you are thinking that they should not, they are thinking that you should. [laughter] As you are thinking they should not do like that, they are thinking you must do that. Then what is it? Difference of opinion. Your vote is single and they are so many. So you have to follow the greatest majority vote. (Lecture on SB 7.9.10, Montreal, 14 July 1968)

He [Śrīla Prabhupāda Bhaktisiddhānta Sarasvatī Gosvāmī Mahārāja] lives forever by his divine instructions and the follower lives with him. (Dedication to *Śrīmad-Bhāgavatam*)

Śrīla Prabhupāda, please accept me as your servant forever.

Dāsābhāsa Bhakti-vikāśa Swami

1998

nama oṁ viṣṇu-pādāya kṛṣṇa-preṣṭhāya bhū-tale
śrīmate bhaktivedānta-svāminn iti nāmine
namas te sārasvate deve gaura-vāṇī-pracāriṇe
nirviśeṣa-śūnyavādi-pāścātya-deśa-tāriṇe

Śrīla Prabhupāda, you are the great *ācārya* whose mission is to save all the souls in the universe. Your drum is now beating in every town and village of the world, and in every stratum of society. Those who are active in that mission glorify you at every moment, for their glorification of Śrī Kṛṣṇa necessarily includes glorification of you, who gave Him to us.

Nevertheless, Vyāsa-*pūjā* is a special day for remembrance and glorification of your divine personality, pastimes, and qualities. Today we shall offer homages, flowers, and feasts, and hopefully many a tear. But maybe the most important offering your direct disciples can make to you is that of the many souls whom we accept as our disciples.

Śrīla Prabhupāda, you told us to "Do as I am doing." Although all of your disciples are highly elevated souls (by your mercy), all of us together cannot add up to even a fraction of what

you are, just as all the *gopīs* together cannot equal Rādhā. Still, we are trying to do as you did, and by your blessings the Kṛṣṇa consciousness movement is becoming more and more successful.

Doing as you did, I also accept disciples. As you were worshiped, I, the most despicable and mean of your disciples, also accept worship. I am certainly not fit to be worshiped; I deserve to be flogged in the streets. I am not fit to chant Hare Kṛṣṇa, or to wear the *tilaka* mark of devotees, or even to have any connection with Kṛṣṇa or His devotees. But you assure me, "Yes, this is what you must do."

Accepting worship seems as antithetical to Vaiṣṇavism as anything could be, but you have taught us this culture, and the Vaiṣṇava secret that goes with it: "Offer everything to guru and Kṛṣṇa. Don't accept anything on your own behalf."

They are singing *saṁsāra-dāvānala-līḍha-loka* ... But it is you, Śrīla Prabhupāda, who receive benediction from the ocean of mercy. It is you who dance in ecstasy in Lord Caitanya's *kīrtana*. It is you who teach Deity worship and enjoy distributing *prasādam*. It is you who relish the pastimes of Śrī Śrī Rādhikā-Mādhava and are expert in assisting the *gopīs* in the groves of Vṛndāvana. It is you who directly represent Kṛṣṇa, and by whose mercy the whole world receives His benediction. It is you, therefore, who are fit to be worshiped as the representative of the Supreme Absolute Truth Personality of Godhead.

Like everything else I have in Kṛṣṇa consciousness, my disciples are gifts from you, entrusted into my care to help keep me engaged in your service. I must offer them back to you, as Gaṅgā is offered to Gaṅgā.

I know nothing, Śrīla Prabhupāda, but what you have taught me—which is everything. I have barely realized a dram of your teachings, but I know they constitute the Absolute Truth. And I know that, by conveying your message to others, they will receive the highest benediction.

My duty is to train my disciples to be worthy followers of the Prabhupāda line. Only if they properly represent you can I happily present them to you. My success will be in training them to practice Kṛṣṇa consciousness as you taught it, and to teach them to recognize your unique and unsurpassable position as the founder-*ācārya* of the International Society for Krishna Consciousness, the vehicle through which Lord Caitanya's inner desires (*mano-'bhīṣṭam*) are to be fulfilled.

This eulogy will take shape not only as writing on paper, but in the words, actions, and thoughts of my disciples. Therefore I am presenting some guidelines so that my disciples may become true Prabhupādānugas. I desire that my disciples:

(1) Be staunch followers of Śrīla Prabhupāda in example and precept;

(2) Be convinced that Kṛṣṇa is the Supreme Personality of Godhead;

(3) Preach this message with full vigor and confidence;

(4) Become learned in Śrīla Prabhupāda's books;

(5) Follow the process of *sādhana* given by Śrīla Prabhupāda;

(6) Be ideal examples of Vaiṣṇava behavior and dealings;

(7) Not be rascals and renege on their initiation vows;

(9) Become attached to the holy names of Kṛṣṇa, both in *japa* and *kīrtana*;

(10) Not be afraid to present themselves as devotees, both in dress (always wearing Vaiṣṇava dress and *tilaka* and not hiding behind *karmī* appearances, unless actually necessary) and in principle (not mixing the philosophy with compromises and speculations);

(11) Always remain within Śrīla Prabhupāda's ISKCON, and not go seeking so-called spiritual solutions elsewhere.

Above all, if my disciples become pure devotees of Kṛṣṇa, they can deliver themselves and the whole world by your grace. They can also deliver me from the ocean of offenses and ineptitude that blemishes my life, and help make me worthy to be placed along with them among the flowers at your lotus feet.

Śrīla Prabhupāda, I am your very fallen and lowly servant, battered by *māyā* but ever willing to keep up the fight, by your blessings. Śrīla Prabhupāda, please accept me as an eternal assistant in your mission of bringing millions of *jīvas* to the shelter of Lord Kṛṣṇa's lotus feet. Let me not be a miser in distributing your mercy. I pray that you always protect me from the madness of becoming a usurper and a hypocrite.

Ever desiring the dust of your feet on my head,

The most wretched, *dīna hīna kāṅgāla pāmara,*
Bhakti Vikāśa Swami

1999

nama oṁ viṣṇu-pādāya kṛṣṇa-preṣṭhāya bhū-tale
śrīmate bhaktivedānta-svāminn iti nāmine
namas te sārasvate deve gaura-vāṇī-pracāriṇe
nirviśeṣa-śūnyavādi-pāścātya-deśa-tāriṇe

Dear Śrīla Prabhupāda,

Most days of the year I offer guru-*pūjā* to you in one of the many temples and preaching centers you have established throughout the world. Nowadays you mostly manifest yourself in these temples in your beautiful deity form, although in some places you still preside from the *vyāsāsana* in your beautiful picture form. In your temples you also manifest as your instructions, your books, and the whole way of life and meaning of life for those who reside there. You also manifest within the hearts of those devotees whose heart's desire is only to please you, and you guide such devotees toward Kṛṣṇa's lotus feet. You guide them by the instructions and inspiration given in your books, and also through the directions given by those of your disciples who have taken up your order to preach and guide others according to your orders.

As I offer you guru-*pūjā*, I try to meditate on at least one of these great gifts you have given us, and on how much you mean to us all. Your guru-*pūjā* is an essential part of the indispensable *sādhana* program you have given us. At guru-*pūjā*, all members of your family come together to acknowledge the gifts you have given us and to confirm your preeminent position in our lives.

Daily as I offer the *ārati* items to you, I resubmit myself as an eternal servitor at your lotus feet. I pray that you guide me and bless me to fulfil the tasks I have set myself in your service. That you are already guiding and blessing me is not denied. You are my guru, and the guru's function is to guide and bless the disciple. Furthermore, if you are not guiding and blessing me, how could I even be in a position to ask your guidance and blessing? Nevertheless, I daily seek your guidance and blessings, knowing that without constantly looking for your mercy, I may become complacent. If I were to think myself not dependent on your mercy, I would again fall into the pit of suffering you so kindly pulled me out of.

I offer the articles one by one, meditating on the limbs of your transcendental body, hearing the prayer composed by Narottama Dāsa Ṭhākura that so aptly and ecstatically describes your divine qualities. I am so small before you, yet my feelings of insignificance mix with the happiness and sense of security that stem from my understanding that you have accepted me. You know my faults and pretensions, yet you have accepted me into your shelter.

You want me to be purified. That I am not, even after so many years of at least superficially following your instructions, demonstrates my lack of sincerity and purpose. Yet, you still do not reject me. My happiness in having such a merciful master mixes with the shame of not serving you properly. Yet still I prostrate myself before you daily and pray that at least during this day may my thoughts and activities be properly centered on you.

In submitting myself to you, Śrīla Prabhupāda, and begging for your mercy, I cannot but think that you want something from me also. You want me to be your worthy representative and thus become a suitable candidate for manifesting your mercy in the world. Please bless me in this way, Śrīla Prabhupāda. Please allow me to attend your guru-*pūjā* every day for eternity, and please make me an instrument in your mission to spread Kṛṣṇa consciousness to every home and heart in the world. It is your desire that not a single living entity in the universe be bereft of Kṛṣṇa consciousness.

And it is our desire, as your disciples, that you be properly honored for establishing ISKCON to give everyone the chance to be Kṛṣṇa conscious. We want there to be thousands upon

thousands of temples of your International Society for Krishna Consciousness, in which thousands upon thousands of devotees will assemble together daily to roar their hearts in appreciation: "*Jaya* Śrīla Prabhupāda!"

Śrīla Prabhupāda, the seed of this Vyāsa-*pūjā* offering manifested in my mind while offering guru-*pūjā* to you on your Vyāsa-*pūjā* day 1998 in Zagreb, Croatia, in a hall packed with several hundred devotees. Śrīla Prabhupāda, I am very happy to report to you that your desires for the spreading of Kṛṣṇa consciousness are gradually being fulfilled, even in places where it was not previously thought possible.

As I compose this offering, I have just returned from a preaching tour in South India. I witnessed Pejawar Swami, the venerable pontiff of the Mādhva *sampradāya,* publicly declare that "ISKCON is the only organization capable of spreading *Viṣṇu-bhakti* throughout the world." And in the many prominent Śrī Vaiṣṇava temples we visited, the *brāhmaṇa* priests, without fail, recognized and honored us as members of your great society because of its unprecedented work in spreading Kṛṣṇa consciousness.

Śrīla Prabhupāda, your society is now facing severe challenges that during the innocent days of your personal presence we could not have imagined. Nevertheless, seeing the tremendous effect your movement is having throughout the world, and how the process of Kṛṣṇa consciousness is the endurably simple, sweet panacea for the world's problems, we are confident that, by your continued blessings, this vitally important Kṛṣṇa consciousness movement will persist in expanding its essential work throughout the world.

Śrīla Prabhupāda, please keep me always in your movement. May my days and lives go on eternally with guru-*pūjā* and guru-*sevā.*

All glories to your lotus feet, Śrīla Prabhupāda!

Your servant eternally,
Bhakti Vikāśa Swami

2000

My dear Śrīla Prabhupāda,

Please accept my humble obeisances in the dust of your lotus feet.

nama oṁ viṣṇu-pādāya kṛṣṇa-preṣṭhāya bhū-tale
śrīmate bhaktivedānta-svāminn iti nāmine
namas te sārasvate deve gaura-vāṇī-pracāriṇe
nirviśeṣa-śūnyavādi-pāścātya-deśa-tāriṇe

Vyāsa-*pūjā* is meant for glorification. However, the past year has seen previously unthinkable offenses being made to you, Śrīla Prabhupāda, from within your own house, ISKCON. Without redress of these offenses, glorification is superficial and hypocritical. Therefore I am restricting this offering to reconfirmation of my position as your eternal servant who wants nothing to do with any minimizing or questioning of your self-effulgent glories.

May those who cling to your lotus feet ever be rewarded with the nectar of your service. And may those who dare blaspheme you also get their just rewards.

Your eternal servant,

Bhakti Vikāśa Swami

[I did not submit an offering in 2001]

Introduction to 2002 Vyāsa-pūjā Book

Impersonalists (the pounding of whom was Śrīla Prabhupāda's pleasure sport) consider words inadequate to describe the truth, and thus meaningless. Actually, the words of impersonalists *are* meaningless. Unfortunately, they do not shut up but continue to spout their meaningless prattle.

Devotees also admit the insufficiency of words to define the truth. Still, understanding the *ānanda* of the truth to be not simply a vague sensation but intimate exchanges of love, devotees employ the choicest of words to glorify the Supreme Absolute Truth, who is the supreme loving person. A love that is transcendental and unsullied is indeed the essence of the Absolute, and although words cannot suffice to praise Him, He nevertheless lovingly accepts sincere attempts to glorify Him.

As a bona fide *ācārya* in the line of Vyāsa, Śrīla Prabhupāda has clearly proved that the Supreme is Kṛṣṇa, the all-loving person who exists simply to love, and who instructs that love of Him can never be complete without love of His loved ones, and that the worship of His devotees is even more important than worship of Himself (*mad-bhakta-pūjābhyadhikā*).

Śrīla Prabhupāda's Vyāsa-*pūjā* festival is thus dear not only to Śrīla Prabhupāda's followers but to Kṛṣṇa Himself, for it is solely meant for honoring this greatest of Kṛṣṇa's ambassadors of love. Although worship of the guru may seem irrelevant to the uninformed, excessive to parochial religionists, and repugnant to the envious, profuse praise of the guru is indeed proper, fitting, and absolutely concordant with the gratefulness due one's savior. Certainly all bona fide delegates of Vyāsa are to be glorified, but Śrīla Prabhupāda should be extraordinarily glorified, for he is a guru extraordinaire. He inherited Lord

Caitanya's gift of being able to give Kṛṣṇa immediately even to most wretched persons devoid of any spiritual qualification. And so although generally a person has to be highly qualified before even beginning to approach Kṛṣṇa (*vīta-rāga-bhaya-krodhāḥ; yeṣāṁ tv anta-gataṁ pāpam; bahūnāṁ janmanām ante*), by the grace of Śrīla Prabhupāda even the most unqualified wretches all over the world were given the chance to approach the Lord.

Śrīla Prabhupāda's Vyāsa-*pūjā* book contains loving glorification of him who brought real love to a world so much lacking it, who was himself full of love, and who taught and practically demonstrated by his very life how to love the all-lovable Lord Śrī Kṛṣṇa by being fully surrendered to Him in loving devotional service.

Within this book are offerings from devotees on various levels of maturity, commitment, and advancement. Submissions by the famous names of ISKCON, seasoned savants and generals who personally saw and interacted with Śrīla Prabhupāda, appear alongside those by devotees whose names and, in some cases, even the cities they preach in are hardly known. Śrīla Prabhupāda's Vyāsa-*pūjā* book contains many sincere prayers; a few literary gems; many personal realizations; anecdotes of Śrīla Prabhupāda's pastimes; narrations of Śrīla Prabhupāda's interactions with devotees even today; news of preaching successes and setbacks; and much more. And because Śrīla Prabhupāda's movement is inextricably linked to and nondifferent from His Divine Grace, this Vyāsa-*pūjā* book also inevitably reflects current events and attitudes within ISKCON.

Like the Supreme Lord he represents, Śrīla Prabhupāda defies comprehensive description. Nevertheless, his direct disciples and his granddisciples have attempted in their own ways to express what Śrīla Prabhupāda means to them. Devotees who take the time to immerse themselves in these realizations cannot but be moved by the love for Śrīla Prabhupāda and his beloved Kṛṣṇa that pervades this volume and is the very meaning of the Vyāsa-*pūjā* book and celebration.

Bhakti-vikāsa Swami

2002

nama oṁ viṣṇu-pādāya kṛṣṇa-preṣṭhāya bhū-tale
śrīmate bhaktivedānta-svāminn iti nāmine
namas te sārasvate deve gaura-vāṇī-pracāriṇe
nirviśeṣa-śūnyavādi-pāścātya-deśa-tāriṇe

Śrīla Prabhupāda, I'm not as outgoing or dynamic as I could be. In a world that needs Kṛṣṇa now, I spend considerable time sitting—reading, writing, and reflecting. You described that you had built the "skyscraper framework" of the Kṛṣṇa consciousness movement and that we, your disciples, should fill it in. But to do that effectively requires more than merely supplying building materials. Even if the framework is firm, to affix poor-quality bricks or add good-quality bricks without having proper knowledge of construction may result in a structure that, albeit large, is yet dysfunctional and possibly even dangerous, rather than a facility in which the whole world can live safely and securely.

Considering this, I have been investigating the nature of the materials that build the house of *bhakti* in this world. With your teachings as the basis, I am researching and gradually writing books on the principles and details of *varṇāśrama-dharma*, *sādhana-bhakti*, Vaiṣṇava behavior, guru-disciple relationships, and other important topics. Obliged to teach others, on your order I also travel, preaching what I have learned from you, as you have taught us to do.

Śrīla Prabhupāda, please help me gain realization of how to appropriately apply your instructions in this complex world. Please bless me with good intelligence and competent assistance so that I may quickly complete these writing projects. Moreover, please bless me with a long life so that I may help in practically demonstrating these concepts in action, thereby further bringing to fruition your dream of a Kṛṣṇa conscious world.

Ever desiring your service, I remain
Your apprentice,
Bhakti Vikāsa Swami

2003

nama oṁ viṣṇu-pādāya kṛṣṇa-preṣṭhāya bhū-tale
śrīmate bhaktivedānta-svāminn iti nāmine
namas te sārasvate deve gaura-vāṇī-pracāriṇe
nirviśeṣa-śūnyavādi-pāścātya-deśa-tāriṇe

Śrīla Prabhupāda, there are innumerable ways in which you can be glorified. In this offering I want to focus on what you have done for me, and who and what I am in relation to you. To others it may seem egoistic that I write about myself, but this offering is meant primarily for you and only marginally for others.

Śrīla Prabhupāda, the more I attempt to glorify you, the more I realize how extraordinarily great you are and how totally insignificant and miniscule I am. Thus I more and more appreciate your extraordinary mercy to have engaged in your mission someone as low as myself. Who am I to act as a spiritual leader, to go from place to place and speak about the most exalted, purest-of-the-pure Lord Śrī Kṛṣṇa? It would be more fitting that I be beaten with shoes and rejected from any assembly of pious persons. Instead, I am often offered honor and respect. But that is only because of my relationship with you, Śrīla Prabhupāda, for I am a very ordinary person from a very ordinary background of lust, sin, and illusion. Devotees are so kind to me due to my connection with you, as I happened to be one of the many persons sprinkled with drops from the tremendous ocean of mercy you so kindly brought. Devotees honor me and tolerate my many faults and insufficiencies because I am yours. I was and am a crow, but you are making me dance like a peacock.

As you yourself wrote in utmost humility:

> You say that before meeting me you could not read or write, so this is all Krishna's grace. If He likes, He can make a crow into a peacock. That is His grace. Krishna consciousness is so valuable that it plays wonderful, and there are many instances within our society. Similarly I was a crow, and now they consider me a peacock. But, I was trying to be a peacock whenever there was the opportunity. I took the endeavor to publish the "Back to Godhead," but I wasted so much time. Ultimately Krishna saved me. (Letter to Haṁsadūta Prabhu, 14 November, 1974)

Śrīla Prabhupāda, you have made me an example of how your extraordinary potency can act through even the most unlikely instruments. My realization is meager: because you want me to repeat your message, I must strive to do so. And my speaking does have some effect, for at least a few listen and feel benefited. Yet I know it cannot be my potency or realization that is affecting them, for I have virtually none. It must be that you, Śrīla Prabhupāda, are working through me.

Śrīla Prabhupāda, I don't want to compete with you. Such an attempt would anyway be impossible, for competition can only be between equals or near-equals. Of course I could make a show of being as realized as you, or nearly as realized as you—or even more advanced! Crazy as it may sound, there will always be enough gullible fools to comprise the supporting cast in such a farce. In the past some of your disciples have enacted such dramas, even successfully for some time, until finally being pummeled into infamy and degradation. So let it be clear that I am a struggling neophyte, clinging to your lotus feet as my only hope. You are the great personage chosen by Lord Caitanya to fulfil His heart's desire of *kīrtana* all over the world. You are uniquely great even among *mahā-bhāgavatas*. If I am able to give any illumination to others, it is as stars reflect the sun. If I properly represent you as an emissary, that is my glory.

Dear Śrīla Prabhupāda, it seems most unlikely that in this lifetime I will develop as an accomplished scholar, musician, singer, expert manager, or great preacher; nor do I have much aptitude for Deity worship or cooking. Here I am struggling to chant sixteen rounds, so what should I hope to achieve? Nevertheless, a real disciple is he who has embraced the spirit of service, so I must do my utmost to serve you as well as I can, despite my incompetence, and without being carried away by delusions of grandeur if my efforts sometimes yield success. Śrīla Prabhupāda, please guide me to discriminate between what is possible for me and what is not, what is required for me and what is not, and please engage me eternally in the service of your mission.

yogyatā-vicāre, kichu nāhi pāi,
tomāra karuṇā—sāra

> In examining my eligibility for devotional service, I find none. Therefore your mercy is essential.

Śrīla Prabhupāda, you echoed these words of Śrīla Bhaktivinoda Ṭhākura by presenting yourself as one of us:

> Actually we are all conditioned souls so our demand from Krishna to accept us is unreasonable. From my personal point of view, I think that I am so sinful that I cannot even approach

> Krishna to show me any favor. But I have only one hope—my Spiritual Master—he is very kind. So someway or other he is dragging me towards Krishna. That is the only hope. Sri Caitanya Caritamrta says therefore: Guru Krishna. By the mercy of the Spiritual Master, and by the mercy of Krishna, one gets into Krishna Consciousness. Narada Muni is our original Spiritual Master and he has dragged so many fallen souls towards Krishna, and we are also hoping to be dragged by Him through the disciplic succession. Otherwise, if we study our own qualifications, there is none—rather I have got so many disqualifications. (Letter to Brahmānanda Prabhu, 10 March 1969)

Śrīla Prabhupāda, you certainly possess all transcendental qualities, among them the extraordinary humility to pray as if devoid of good qualities. But such self-deprecation is actually suitable for a fallen soul like myself. So let me always remember those words of yours and my actual position in relationship to you and your dearmost Lord Kṛṣṇa, lest I think of myself according to what others say about me: "sadhu," "scholar," "fundamentalist," and so on. Of course, I am not worthy of such compliments, but it is a fact that the process for self-realization you have given us is so exalted, especially in comparison to the fallen condition of the world today, that if anyone simply tries to follow your instructions and repeat them to others, it will surely be appreciated at least by devotionally inclined persons. Śrīla Prabhupāda, I pray for the spiritual strength and equilibrium of mind to remain in your service till the time of leaving this body, and beyond. And though it is not at all necessary that I be remembered after my departure, nevertheless should anyone care to do so, then I aspire that it not be as a "sadhu," "scholar," or whatever. My glory and the fulfillment of my life will be if others say, "He was a faithful servant of Śrīla Prabhupāda. He genuinely believed in the words of his spiritual master."

Śrīla Prabhupāda, a godbrother of yours once told me, "My guru was like a lion, your guru was like a lion, and you should also be like a lion." Considering that lions do not give birth to rabbits, I am trying to be your worthy disciple by repeating your words and speaking strongly as you did—for which some members of your movement criticize me: "Who are you to talk like that? We have seen so many hardliners talk big, big things, only to fall down and make fools of themselves. What is the guarantee that you also won't fall down?" In reply I may contend, "Undoubtedly it is true that if ever I were to disconnect myself from the lotus feet of Śrīla Prabhupāda, then that act in itself would render me fallen. But although I and thousands of others may come and go, Śrīla Prabhupāda and his instructions will stay; and those who remain faithful to those instructions will triumph over the material energy. Śrīla Prabhupāda's words are always glorious, and so is the endeavor to glorify Śrīla Prabhupāda by repeating them. I am certainly not fit to do so; I agree that it is simply my impudence in doing so. But *śāstra* states that the disciple should praise the guru and repeat his instructions. So why should I deny my desire to glorify Śrīla Prabhupāda? If you think that I will fall down, then better I take this opportunity to glorify Śrīla Prabhupāda now, before my intelligence becomes spoiled. Certainly I must unceasingly pray to Śrīla Prabhupāda to purify my consciousness by constant meditation on his lotus feet. And if I follow his instructions carefully and don't commit offenses, then I can stick tightly to his lotus feet without falling away. Fit or unfit, I must endeavor to speak, write, and be purified. Though my words may be infected with nasty consciousness, madness, lethargy, duplicity, dullness, desire for name and fame, anger, envy, immaturity, anarchy, *tamo-guṇa, rajo-guṇa,* maybe a little *sattva-guṇa,* and millions of inauspicious qualities piled on thickly in innumerable ghastly layers, still I must attempt to repeat what Śrīla Prabhupāda said. That is glorification of

Śrīla Prabhupāda and is automatically auspicious. I must try to glorify Śrīla Prabhupāda despite my inability."

Śrīla Prabhupāda, please keep me engaged in your service and in the service of your servants, while always remembering my actual position:

jagāi mādhāi haite muñi se pāpiṣṭha
purīṣera kīṭa haite muñi se laghiṣṭha

I am a worse sinner than Jagāi and Mādhāi and am lower than worms in stool.

Praying to be your *dāsa* eternally,
Bhakti Vikāśa Swami

2004

nama oṁ viṣṇu-pādāya kṛṣṇa-preṣṭhāya bhū-tale
śrīmate bhaktivedānta-svāminn iti nāmine
namas te sārasvate deve gaura-vāṇī-pracāriṇe
nirviśeṣa-śūnyavādi-pāścātya-deśa-tāriṇe

Śrīla Prabhupāda, I worship you by attempting to present your message to others without change. Others may dilute or distort your teachings but I shall not. I believe this is the best way to worship you and indeed that anything less than this is not actual worship but only a hypocritical show that cannot be satisfying to you. Please make me your instrument, however tiny, in your mission of kicking out cheating religion from the world, beginning from within your own house.

Wishing to be accepted as your genuine servant,
Bhakti Vikāsa Svāmī*

---

* Submitted for inclusion in but not featured in the Vyāsa-*pūjā* book of 2004.

2005

nama oṁ viṣṇu-pādāya kṛṣṇa-preṣṭhāya bhū-tale
śrīmate bhaktivedānta-svāminn iti nāmine
namas te sārasvate deve gaura-vāṇī-pracāriṇe
nirviśeṣa-śūnyavādi-pāścātya-deśa-tāriṇe

In Calcutta on 16 Āśvina, 1337 (Bengali calendar, corresponding to 23 October 1930), His Divine Grace Śrīla Bhaktisiddhānta Sarasvatī Ṭhākura spoke the following:

> Our *gurudeva* was not an instructor in any subject concerned with enjoyment of this material world. Again, he was the sole unmistaking judge of all topics of this world. But I am deprived and fallen; because of my weakness not everything Śrī Gurudeva said entered my heart. But let me have millions of tongues and millions of heads to repeat whatever entered my ear by his mercy, and a lifespan of millions of years in unlimited universes for broadcasting descriptions of his incomparable, nonharmful compassion. That will be my guru-*pūjā*. He will be satisfied, and being pleased will shower unlimited benediction, by which I will be able to broadcast descriptions of his mercy with even more millions of tongues. On that day I will get relief from the glorification of all topics concerned with this destructible illusion, and from all kinds of mundane education within the universe.

Like one offering Mandākinī to the Gaṅgā, I offer the above quote at the lotus feet of His Divine Grace Śrīla A.C. Bhaktivedanta Swami Prabhupāda, who is fulfilling the desires of his own most worshipable *gurudeva* by preaching his message and glories throughout the universe.

Śrīla Prabhupāda, please be pleased with my attempt to glorify your *gurudeva*. By that attempt may you be all the more glorified, and thus grant me the benediction to be able to eternally glorify the lotus-foot dust of our *ācāryas.*

Offered with prayers for your mercy—which is indispensible for me—by the most miserable

Bhakti Vikāsa Swami

2006

nama oṁ viṣṇu-pādāya kṛṣṇa-preṣṭhāya bhū-tale
śrīmate bhaktivedānta-svāminn iti nāmine
namas te sārasvate deve gaura-vāṇī-pracāriṇe
nirviśeṣa-śūnyavādi-pāścātya-deśa-tāriṇe

Śrīla Prabhupāda, I am completely dependent on your mercy. "Completely" means completely. Not 90% or 99.9% or 99.999%. Completely: 100%. I have no ability or strength or intelligence of my own. Whatever I am in Kṛṣṇa consciousness is due only to your mercy. And my many failings are simply my own nonsense.

Due to my own offensiveness and unwillingness, I haven't gone very far in devotional service, and that I am still on the path is due only to your mercifully not kicking me away, as I deserve, but keeping me engaged. All my attempts in *sādhana,* preaching, and other endeavors in Kṛṣṇa's service, depend entirely on your mercy, without which I am nothing. Only if imbued with your mercy can my activities be successful.

Realization of dependence on the guru's mercy naturally arises early in the spiritual career of a disciple, so it might seem strange that I am expressing such a sentiment after a relatively long period in your service. These feelings are not new to me, but recently struck me afresh as I was considering how some of my disciples—flowers whom you have sent to be prepared for offering to Kṛṣṇa—apparently feel toward me. They may think I am great and wonderful, but I am not. Śrīla Prabhupāda, you are great and wonderful.

Remembering your greatness and my smallness keeps me safe under the shelter of your lotus feet. For me to accept disciples is certainly risky, but if I just remember that your mercy is all that I am made of, and that my duty is to transmit that mercy to others, then I will remain safe. I am inadequate, but you carry what I lack and preserve it—by your mercy.

Happily bowing down at your lotus feet, I pray millions of times to be your truly humble servant,

Bhakti Vikāsa Swami

2007

nama oṁ viṣṇu-pādāya kṛṣṇa-preṣṭhāya bhū-tale
śrīmate bhaktivedānta-svāminn iti nāmine
namas te sārasvate deve gaura-vāṇī-pracāriṇe
nirviśeṣa-śūnyavādi-pāścātya-deśa-tāriṇe

Śrīla Prabhupāda, when you were personally manifest in our presence, it was clear to most of your disciples that even though some were relatively senior and advanced, in comparison to you we were all micromidgets. Your position was exceptional, even among your godbrothers.

Nothing has changed. You are simply the best. There is no comparison with what you have done and how you continue to profoundly influence innumerable people. Without disrespect to the many sincere souls practicing Kṛṣṇa consciousness and trying to follow in your footsteps, your extraordinariness remains axiomatically unique for those sane enough to acknowledge it.

Although it is impossible to fully understand or describe what makes you so outstanding even among saints, one major aspect is your intense desire to please guru and Kṛṣṇa, which manifests through your unflagging attempts to awaken every living being to his real identity as an eternal servant of Kṛṣṇa and to cultivate even the slightest inclination he might have toward acting in that capacity. Moreover, despite being so far above all, you consider yourself not master but servant of everyone. You are totally selfless. You have given yourself to guru and Kṛṣṇa and are one with their desire to give Kṛṣṇa to every *jīva* in the universe. You are certainly in a category apart from those who foolishly advertise or imply themselves to be more realized or intelligent than you.

As a fully surrendered servant of the *paramparā*, you never compromise for the sake of pleasing the public or gaining cheap fame or popularity. Nor do you exploit disciples to fulfil personal desires. Nor do you act the role of what others think a sadhu or *premī-bhakta* should be, but are always naturally and unaffectedly absorbed in serving Kṛṣṇa. For these and innumerable other reasons, I feel so fortunate and grateful that Kṛṣṇa sent you, and no one else, to be my guru.

To earn your blessings and properly glorify you requires imbibing your quality of wholly guileless sincerity. Neither flattery, sentimental or fanatical adulation, or formal praise can fool or satisfy you. It seems impossible to attain the standard of Kṛṣṇa consciousness that you have exemplified, but it is easy because you make it easy; that is your mercy. And that we are entirely dependent on your mercy is not simply a platitude, as evidenced by the various litters of tigers-by-your-mercy now reconverted into mice.

You are a genuine *mahā-bhāgavata,* an empowered representative of Kṛṣṇa fully capable of bestowing His mercy upon all conditioned souls and thus delivering them back to His lotus feet. Even though I am one of the most severely contaminated persons upon whom your merciful glance has fallen, you are so kind that you engage me in the exalted service of delivering your message so that others may attain the divine grace you so mercifully distribute.

I pray to always treasure these simple, quintessential, and powerful truths, upon which all our spiritual endeavors depend. Remembering your warning to protect the valuable jewel of spiritual love from thieves and burglars, and being increasingly surrounded by pseudo intellectuals, diluters, and committed doubters, I cling to the lifeline of my connection with you, without which whatever little Kṛṣṇa consciousness I have imbibed is doomed.

Śrīla Prabhupāda, to aspire to be your servant is no small thing. Even great demigods and the inhabitants of Vaikuṇṭha can hardly recognize the value of such a position or become eligible for it. Yet you have planted in this otherwise thoroughly disqualified person the desire for eternal service at your lotus feet. Indeed, only you and Kṛṣṇa know how severely disqualified I am for such a boon; and only you and Kṛṣṇa are merciful and powerful enough to nonetheless make me worthy and fulfil my aspiration.

Bhakti Vikāsa Swami

2008

Dear Śrīla Prabhupāda,

Please accept my most respectful and grateful obeisances in the dust of your divine lotus feet.

Among the innumerable priceless gifts you have given us is daily recitation during *brāhma-muhūrta* of the enchantingly sweet *Śrī Gurv-aṣṭaka*. Through this divine offering by Śrīla Viśvanātha Cakravartī Ṭhākura to his *gurudeva*, he has wonderfully summarized the quintessential qualities of all Gauḍīya *mahānta*-gurus.

Yet from my plane, it seems that some of the stanzas of *Śrī Gurv-aṣṭaka* particularly describe Your Divine Grace. For example, Śrīla Cakravartīpāda begins by acclaiming the guru's mercy, and I, being *saṁsāra-dāvānala-līḍha* and hence particularly in need of mercy, naturally reflect that among the many *mahānta*-gurus who have come to this world to assist Lord Caitanya in spreading Kṛṣṇa consciousness, you are the one who superlatively and uniquely rained down His mercy of pure elixir—the only genuine antidote for the forest fire of material existence—brought directly from the auspicious ocean of transcendental qualities.

After describing throughout the next six verses some of your prominent divine characteristics, in the last stanza Śrīla Cakravartīpāda again indicates the crucial significance of your mercy. Guru-*kṛpā* is essential even for elevated souls, but for us Western barbarians—whom you ministered to with extraordinary compassion—its significance is multiplied exponentially. As you ascertained, the people on this planet have no capacity for any type of austerity, and are neither very capable of study nor very pious; the only thing they are able to do is somehow take shelter at your feet. Simply by a little smile from your benevolent lotus lips, Kṛṣṇa's mercy is attained and the whole spiritual realm is opened to us. But without your mercy, then however else we attempt to please Kṛṣṇa, we remain forever cut off from Him.

Mercy (*prasāda*) is also the subject of the fourth stanza, which describes distribution of sanctified food, an activity central to your mission. Gauḍīya gurus prevenient to Your Divine Grace tended to emphasize Lord Caitanya's instruction *bhālo nā khāibe:* "Do not eat nicely." But on indication from Śrīla Cakravartīpāda, you found in *prasāda* a merciful means to bring persons of the lowest level of consciousness, *anna-maya,* to the highest, *ānanda-maya.* You personally relished *śrī-bhagavat-prasāda* and happily arranged that your disciples and the whole world do so.

We also saw you jumping and dancing while relishing the mellows of *mahāprabhoḥ kīrtana*, and eagerly, constantly, and unlimitedly glorifying Śrī Rādhikā-Mādhava—and serving Them in Their enchanting Deity forms with devotion so manifest that even a stonehearted soul like myself could understand that you are on the same platform as Hari (*sākṣād-dharitvena*) and very dear to Him (*kintu prabhor yaḥ priyaḥ*).

The Vaiṣṇavas' mercy is always available to those who sincerely beg for it, so on this occasion I crave from you the boon to forever glorify you through *Śrī Gurv-aṣṭaka.* Śrīla Cakravartīpāda offers to those who recite this prayer the blessing of direct service to Kṛṣṇa in Vṛndāvana. So I hopefully and eagerly anticipate that, despite my being wretched and disqualified, you will ultimately take my hand and lead me to the groves of Śrī Vraja-*dhāma* to eternally assist you in serving the Divine Couple. I am still very, very far—seemingly impossibly far—from being fit for such a boon, but am confident that just as you have lifted me up from the gutter and engaged me in devotional service, you can take me all the way back to Godhead. Right here and now, I am extraordinarily fortunate to be participating in your distribution of mercy within the *saṅkīrtana* mission of *karuṇa-avatāra* Śrī Śacī-nandana Gaura-hari, the combined form of Śrī Rādhā-Mādhava. For all these gifts, we should meditate upon and offer obeisances at your lotus feet not just three times a day but at every moment.

All glories to your lotus feet, Śrīla Prabhupāda. All glories to those of Śrīla Viśvanātha Cakravartī Ṭhākura and to those of all the previous *ācāryas*, the dust of which you have sprinkled upon us. All glories to the supreme object of worship of the Gauḍīyas, Śrī Rādhā-Mādhava in the bowers of Vṛndāvana.

Aspiring for your mercy to attain eternal service therein,

Your otherwise totally unqualified
Bhakti Vikāsa Swami

2009

nama oṁ viṣṇu-pādāya kṛṣṇa-preṣṭhāya bhū-tale
śrīmate bhaktivedānta-svāminn iti nāmine
namas te sārasvate deve gaura-vāṇī-pracāriṇe
nirviśeṣa-śūnyavādi-pāścātya-deśa-tāriṇe

nāma-śresthaṁ manum api śacī-putram atra svarūpaṁ
rūpaṁ tasyāgrajam uru-purīṁ māthurīṁ goṣṭhavāṭīm
rādhā-kuṇḍaṁ giri-varam aho rādhikā-mādhavāśāṁ
prāpto yasya prathita-kṛpayā śrī-guruṁ taṁ nato 'smi

I bow to my spiritual master, by whose profuse mercy I have received the supreme holy name, the divine mantra, the son of Śacī (Lord Caitanya), Svarūpa Damodara, Rūpa Gosvāmī and his older brother Sanātana Gosvāmī, the supreme abode of

> Mathurā, the abode of Vṛndāvana, Rādha-kuṇḍa, Govardhana Hill, and the desire for service to Śrī Rādhikā and Mādhava. (*Muktā-carita*, Śrīla Raghunātha Dāsa Gosvāmī)*

Śrīla Prabhupāda, having completed twenty years attempting to serve you in the *sannyāsa-āśrama*, I must first thank you for giving me the opportunity to render service to you throughout my life by traveling, speaking, writing, and preaching. Of course, ultimately *āśrama* is unimportant in Kṛṣṇa consciousness, and at best I am a castor-plant, Kali-yuga excuse for a *sannyāsī*. Yet I must still thank you for saving me from any black-hole tragedies, for protecting and sustaining me in this difficult *sannyāsa-āśrama*, and for giving me the freedom to preach without concern for personal maintenance and without entanglement from children, wife, home, and the rest.

I am very happy in your service.

ātma-nivedana, tuwā pade kori',
hoinu parama sukhī
duḥkha dūre gelo, cintā nā rohilo,
caudike ānanda dekhi

> I have become supremely happy by surrendering myself at Your lotus feet. Sorrow has gone far away, and worry has not remained. Everywhere I see bliss. (*Śaraṇāgati*, Śrīla Bhaktivinoda Ṭhākura)

Of course, being your sannyasi brings great responsibility. *Sannyāsa* is meant neither for luxurious living nor carefree wandering, but for performing significant service. You wanted your disciples to be recognized for their greatness—not the greatness attained by hype or by collecting sentimentalists and sycophants, nor of attaining a high position from which

* This translation is as I had composed it. Unfortunately, it was rendered differently in the published Vyāsa-*pūjā* book.

to exploit others, but the greatness that follows total surrender and utter humility. Śrīla Prabhupāda, my lack of significant service to your lotus feet, despite having all opportunity to perform it, sadly speaks of my dearth of both surrender and humility. Therefore, on this day I beg your mercy that I may at last rectify myself and serve you as I properly should. May I cast aside all petty ambition and become a true disciple of such a glorious master as Your Divine Grace.

You have given us everything, Śrīla Prabhupāda. Via the Hare Kṛṣṇa mantra you have given us Rādha-Kṛṣṇa and the whole spiritual world:

> Prabhupāda handed [Robert] a small piece of paper with the Hare Kṛṣṇa mantra printed on it.
>
> Robert: While Swamiji was handing it to me, he had this big smile on his face, like he was handing me the world. (*Śrīla Prabhupāda-līlāmṛta*)

Śrīla Prabhupāda, you are the one who can bring me to the spiritual world. You have opened the door, showed me the treasure therein, and commissioned me to bring others also. I attempt to do that by exhorting them to heed your message. In a world dangerously spinning toward pandemonium, your message is urgently needed more than ever, for you have offered all solutions to the myriad confusions facing society—even before others were aware of the problems. There has never been a more vital nor better time for preaching. Throughout the world, people are eager to take your books and hear your message.

Please empower us, for the favorable factors are complicated by innumerable hurdles, not the least of which is the state of your ISKCON—which in essence is nondifferent from you and, being the prime medium of service to you, is the means whereby our relationship with you is maintained and nourished. Vyāsa-*pūjā* offerings are not meant for airing gripes, but I cannot but express concern for your movement. Various compromises and deviations, exacerbated by pronounced leadership problems, are making your house a precarious one in which to live.

The challenges are enormous, and we can overcome them only by invoking your mercy and recalling how you remained steadfast amidst apparently insurmountable obstacles. You triumphed by your full commitment to do the unimaginable: deliver Kṛṣṇa consciousness to a degraded and apathetic populace. Your success formula is the only one that has ever or will ever work in the spiritual sphere: invoking the mercy of the previous *ācāryas* by having full faith in their words and full dependence upon their favor. We too can achieve the impossible by reverting to the same principle, the one you incessantly taught:

guru-mukha-padma-vākya, cittete kariyā aikya,
āra nā kariha mane āśā

Whatever happens, Śrīla Prabhupāda, I want to stay with you. I know that you are always with me, despite my often almost willful forgetfulness of you. I feel your potency charging me when I speak and write; otherwise how could I even dream of speaking and writing for Kṛṣṇa? If you wish, you can make me a vessel for delivering your message in a manner we now can hardly envisage.

Your mercy is all that I am made of. Praying to ever remain in the shelter of your lotus feet, and in that of your true followers,

Bhakti Vikāsa Swami

2010

Śrīla Prabhupāda, I desire to attain your full mercy by placing upon my head the dust of your lotus feet, and thereby receive the concentrated essence of all the mercy of all the Vaiṣṇavas that has ever been available in the history of the universe.

bhakta-pada-dhūli āra bhakta-pada-jala
bhakta-bhukta-avaśeṣa—tina mahā-bala

> The dust of the feet of a devotee, the water that has washed the feet of a devotee, and the remnants of food left by a devotee are three very powerful substances.

ei tina-sevā haite kṛṣṇa-premā haya
punaḥ punaḥ sarva-śāstre phukāriyā kaya

> By rendering service to these three, one attains the supreme goal of ecstatic love for Kṛṣṇa. In all the revealed scriptures this is loudly declared again and again. (Cc *Antya* 16.60–61)

Śrīla Prabhupāda, to receive the dust of your lotus feet on my head would be the ultimate perfection of my existence. But such a benediction is not easily attained. While it might be considered that disciples have an inalienable right to access the mercy of their guru's feet, and although some Māyāvādīs and *prākṛta-sahajiyā* "sadhus" unreservedly bestow their foot-dust even to casual visitors, *ācāryas* of our *paramparā* have been more circumspect.

In your purports to verses 1.17.244–45 of *Caitanya-caritāmṛta*, you have stated:

> This holding of a great personality's lotus feet is certainly very good for the person who takes the dust, but this example of Śrī Caitanya Mahāprabhu's unhappiness indicates that a Vaiṣṇava should not allow anyone to take dust from his feet.

> One who takes the dust of a great personality's lotus feet transfers his sinful activities to that great personality. Unless the person whose dust is taken is very strong, he must suffer the sinful activities of the person who takes the dust. Therefore ordinarily it should not be allowed. Sometimes in big meetings people come to take the same advantage by touching our feet. On account of this, sometimes we have to suffer from some disease. As far as possible, no outsider should be allowed to touch one's feet to take dust from them. Śrī Caitanya Mahāprabhu personally showed this by His example.
>
> Śrī Caitanya Mahāprabhu is God Himself, but He was playing the part of a preacher. Every preacher should know that being allowed to touch a Vaiṣṇava's feet and take dust may be good for the person who takes it, but it is not good for the person who allows it to be taken. As far as possible, this practice should ordinarily be avoided. Only initiated disciples should be allowed to take this advantage, not others. Those who are full of sinful activities should generally be avoided.

Several devotees have confirmed that at least up until around 1970, it was fairly common that disciples and committed newcomers would touch your lotus feet. But that changed. Udayānanda Prabhu recalled that in 1974, when being awarded Gāyatrī mantra by you, he asked permission to touch your lotus feet, and that you smiled and replied, "That is not necessary." By 1975, when I was mercifully accepted into ISKCON, senior devotees would routinely warn juniors not to touch your feet, informing us that you did not like it—which is understandable for a guru who has thousands of disciples.

And only to a fortunate few did Your Divine Grace award the massive benediction of placing your feet upon their head. You once did so in 1968 in Montreal, on the request of the three householder couples whom you had prepared for preaching in England.

The benediction of receiving the dust from the lotus feet of a *mahā-bhāgavata* is so rarely bestowed that apparently some special qualification—beyond formal discipleship—is required for achieving it. As Śrīla Bhaktisiddhānta Sarasvatī once told some respectable ladies of Dacca who had come to worship him and who apparently expected to touch his lotus feet, "For those inclined to freely touch anyone's feet, I recall the words of my *gurudeva*—'Why do they so boldly stretch out their hands to take dust from the feet of a sadhu? Do they really consider themselves sufficiently qualified?'"

Although Śrīla Gaura Kiśora Dāsa Bābājī always strictly forbad anyone to touch his feet, he once voluntarily placed them on Śrī Siddhānta Sarasvatī's head. What was the difference between those who were refused such a benediction, and that personage upon whom it was happily bestowed? What is the qualification to receive the dust of a *mahā-bhāgavata*'s lotus feet?

A great pure devotee such as Your Divine Grace comes to this world only due to causeless mercy, with the sole intention to distribute mercy. Yet, that mercy is bestowed upon some more than others, for not all recipients are equally eager to receive it. Just as a duck who quacks the most insistently is given more food, devotees who sincerely cry out for special mercy thus qualify themselves for it, by dint of their strong desire to be blessed with an opportunity for intimate service.

The devotees who were embarking for London in 1968 were on a mission most dear to you, yet apparently almost impossible to execute. They were attempting to emulate a feat nearly parallel to what Your Divine Grace had accomplished—to go to an unknown country, with no local friends or support and

with very little money, and introduce the foreign culture of Lord Caitanya's *saṅkīrtana* movement. They were six, rather than being alone, as you had been. Unlike in your case, they were backed by a movement (albeit distant, fledgling, and unrecognized), and they also had the example of your prior success.

Still, the likelihood of their success might seem to have been even less than yours was when you set out for America, because they lacked your maturity, your lifelong absorption in the culture and philosophy of Kṛṣṇa consciousness, and your zenith purity.

Both in your going to America and in your householder disciples' venture to England, the crucial asset was total faith in and commitment to fulfil—against all odds—the will of the spiritual master. Such wholehearted faith in the spiritual master, and such determination to execute his order even in the most trying of circumstances, and without considering personal convenience, loss, or gain, is to my understanding the essential qualification for attaining the complete, unreserved mercy of the spiritual master. A true disciple's desire is one with that of his guru. He maintains no doubts about his guru, nor any ambition other than to serve him. And when a spiritual master sees a disciple thus qualified, he voluntarily places his feet on that disciple's head. Then the mercy flows through unobstructed, and the seemingly impossible becomes a reality.

But such mercy is neither cheap nor easily attained. Surely, Śrīla Prabhupāda, the dust of your lotus feet is sought by, yet difficult to achieve, even for great demigods and sages. Only to those who strongly, unfailingly, and guilelessly seek the mercy of a pure devotee is it unreservedly bestowed. Udayānanda Prabhu related how he received your mercy—far beyond his expectation or imagination—in Vṛndāvana in 1977, when you were enacting your pastime of prolonged sickness:

> I had always had this desire to touch the lotus feet of the pure devotee, and this went back to the time when I was getting *brāhmaṇa*-initiated in 1974 and I asked Śrīla Prabhupāda could I touch his feet and Prabhupāda said, "No, that is not necessary." So here I am in Śrīla Prabhupāda's room, and I look over and I see Trivikrama Swami, and he's massaging Prabhupāda's feet. And I'm thinking, "Why is he getting all this mercy?" But then I'm thinking, "Oh, I don't even deserve to be in this room." And then all of a sudden Mahārāja yawned, and I said, "Oh, Kṛṣṇa!" So I humbly came over to Mahārāja and said, "Would it be OK if I took over and massaged Śrīla Prabhupāda's feet?" And he said, "OK." I thought, "Oh, my God, I don't believe this is really going to happen!" So then Mahārāja took me over and he showed me. So I was so gentle, and I was massaging the lotus feet of Śrīla Prabhupāda, and I got to massage him for two-and-a-half hours. Then at one point Prabhupāda looked up and said, "Who is massaging my feet?" Tamāla Kṛṣṇa Mahārāja said, "Oh, that's Udayānanda Dāsa." And Prabhupāda said, "Oh." And then there was this smile on Prabhupāda's face as if after all these years he was fulfilling my desire. Then by the mercy of Śrīla Prabhupāda, he allowed me to massage his feet every day for the next three weeks. But I was thinking that I was the most fortunate soul in the whole universe at that time.

My dear Śrīla Prabhupāda, I most woefully deprive myself of your full mercy by not strongly enough desiring it. Although it is available to all, I have not taken it. Examining myself after all these years of supposedly preaching Kṛṣṇa consciousness, I cannot but admit that I am still nurturing insane hopes for sense gratification. I am simply a pretender. Yet while lamenting my foolishness and hypocrisy, I must recognize that by your mercy there also exists within my heart a desire to be done forever with all my nonsense and to thus become your actual disciple.

Śrīla Prabhupāda, notwithstanding my stupidity and knowing myself to be unqualified, I sustain the wish that you just once place your lotus feet on my head—this storehouse of wretched thoughts—and thus award me the kind of purification that cannot be attained throughout millions of lifetimes of other practices, not even by assiduously performing *sādhana-bhakti*. By the mercy of your feet, I will receive the mercy of all previous *ācāryas*, and of *sādvaitaṁ sāvadhūtaṁ parijana-sahitaṁ kṛṣṇa-caitanya-devaṁ/ śrī-rādhā-kṛṣṇa-pādān saha-gaṇa-lalitā-śrī-viśākhānvitāṁś ca*. Such an opportunity is worth waiting millions of lifetimes for. I might not qualify for that mercy very soon, but the hope of attaining it keeps me alive—though blundering—in service at your lotus feet. Praying to always have a place there,

your aspiring servant,
Bhakti Vikāsa Swami

2011

nama oṁ viṣṇu-pādāya kṛṣṇa-preṣṭhāya bhū-tale
śrīmate bhaktivedānta-svāminn iti nāmine
namas te sārasvate deve gaura-vāṇī-pracāriṇe
nirviśeṣa-śūnyavādi-pāścātya-deśa-tāriṇe

Śrīla Prabhupāda, only a fool would consider you anything less than a topmost perfect *paramahaṁsa*, an ambassador from the spiritual world, a personal representative of Kṛṣṇa. For one blessed with the eyes to see, everything about you evidences your extraordinary love for Kṛṣṇa. As is profusely and lovingly described in this *Vyāsa-pūjā* book, you are abundantly decorated with all the symptoms of a pure devotee.

Yet you defy the pathetic, disgusting stereotype of a saintly person who wears a dreamy smile and is perpetually "nice."

Your unfathomable love for Kṛṣṇa is manifest not simply by talking of love, compassion, and other such exalted virtues, but more realistically in your down-to-earth, service-oriented example—which defies the listlessness of so-called *premī-bhaktas,* whose reputations rest on their narrating of *gopī-līlās,* bathing in Rādhā-kuṇḍa, and other such esoterica. You demonstrated in practice how a devotee who loves Kṛṣṇa strives against all opposition to establish His glories in this world. You did not care for reputation; you simply wanted to serve the order of your guru. Anyone who reads your books can readily understand that you are not at all sentimental, vague, or wishy-washy. You are a natural, unaffected saint, not an actor dancing according to the expectations of mindless people. Indeed, your profound compassion for the rebellious *jīvas* often manifested as extraordinarily forceful attacks upon their foolishness and rascaldom.

Among the many transcendental characteristics that distinguish you as the *jagad-guru* (Kṛṣṇa's selected emissary to this world), in my mind one towers above all: your unmitigated, uncompromisable commitment to defeat the enemies of your beloved Kṛṣṇa. You especially targeted the *nirviśeṣa-vādīs,* who attempt to belittle Kṛṣṇa by denying that He is categorically superior, in every respect, to all other living beings (*nirviśeṣa* literally means "not special"), who claim latent or already attained parity with Kṛṣṇa, and whose mystic-sounding ambiguities are extolled as realized spirituality by persons so overwhelmingly insincere as to be attracted to such charlatans.

Śrīla Prabhupāda, that you left Vṛndāvana to contest Māyāvāda amid the nastiness of America is a more convincing testimony to your love for Kṛṣṇa than had you stayed in Vṛndāvana. Your *praṇāma-mantra,* composed by yourself, describes what you considered to be the essence of your mission: service to

Śrīla Bhaktisiddhānta Sarasvatī (*sārasvate deve*) on this plane (*bhū-tale*) by preaching the message of Caitanya Mahāprabhu (*gaura-vāṇī*) and thus saving (*tāriṇe*) the Western countries (*pāścātya-deśa*) from impersonalism and voidism (*nirviśeṣa-śūnyavāda*). Such extraordinary activities could be performed only by a devotee who is exceptionally dear to Kṛṣṇa (*kṛṣṇa-preṣṭha*).

In accord with your mission, and pertinent to the arena and ethos of your service, you emphasized and exemplified more the need to fight for Kṛṣṇa than to discuss His *rāsa-līlā*. For me, one particular anecdote (narrated by Hayagrīva Dāsa in *The Hare Krishna Explosion*) encapsulates your intense devotion to Kṛṣṇa as manifested in *vīra-rasa*.

In 1966, during one of your classes at 26 Second Avenue, after you had criticized Dr. Radhakrishnan's comment that it is not to the personal Kṛṣṇa that we must surrender but to "the unborn, beginningless, eternal who speaks through Kṛṣṇa," you added, "This Māyāvādī philosophy is worse than atheism." Thereupon Keith, the Mott Street denim-clad "guru" (later initiated as Kīrtanānanda Dāsa), launched a long spiel in defense of Dr. Radhakrishnan and Māyāvāda. He rambled on about the "Self and the One Mind," quoting Śaṅkara and Huang Po, Buddha and Christ, Spinoza and St. Paul, while you, "Swamiji," sat on the dais, your complexion turning red. After Keith finally wound down, you asked him:

> "So, you have understood what we have been saying—that Kṛṣṇa is God?"
>
> "Yes," Keith says.
>
> "And that worship is due God?"
>
> "Yes," Keith says.

> Suddenly Swamiji, red and furious, stands up. "Then why do you want to take it away from Kṛṣṇa?" he roars, shaking the small storefront. "It's Kṛṣṇa! It's Kṛṣṇa!" He slams his hand down on the lectern. "It's no unborn within Kṛṣṇa! It's Kṛṣṇa!" We all sit stunned, as if a lion had pounced on the dais. "Kṛṣṇa, the Supreme Personality of Godhead, is directly telling Arjuna, 'To Me. Worship Me.' And Dr. Radhakrishnan says that it is not to the person Kṛṣṇa but to some void. Just see what a nonsense rascal! Do you want to worship some unborn void instead of Kṛṣṇa? Kṛṣṇa is the Absolute Truth. His body, mind, and self are absolute. And He says, 'Think of Me, be devoted to Me, worship Me.' And even Śaṅkara says, *bhaja govindaṁ, bhaja govindaṁ, bhaja govindam:* 'Worship Govinda, worship Govinda, worship Govinda. Your nonsense will not save you at death!' And yet this rascal wants to take it away from Kṛṣṇa. Do you want to follow such a rascal? Kṛṣṇa says, 'Worship Me.' Do you not understand? Then why are you saying it is not to Kṛṣṇa? Why? Why not to Kṛṣṇa?" ...
>
> [*Next morning*] "We are declaring war," Swamiji says. "War on *māyā*."

Śrīla Prabhupāda, by declaring war in the storefront, you risked losing your fledgling flock, the only followers (if at that stage they could be considered followers) that you had after several months in America. But you could not brook Māyāvāda. And for that reason Kṛṣṇa was to bless you most extraordinarily.

Śrīla Prabhupāda, please enlist me in your army, without an option to retire. I beg for the benediction to be eternally engaged in your mission. May I be prepared to go anywhere throughout the universe—tolerating the difficulties of heat, cold, hunger, thirst, unpopularity, persecution, or whatever the material energy may throw at me—always happy to follow your orders, knowing that by doing so, Kṛṣṇa will be pleased, and that hence there is nothing better for me to do. Of course, words like these are easy to state yet difficult to fulfil. If I could actually pray in that way from within my heart and be unhesitatingly ready to do anything and everything to serve you under all circumstances, then I might qualify as your genuine servant.

Śrīla Prabhupāda, my words are insufficient to praise you or to in any way approximate a sufficient portrayal of your innumerable divine qualities. Even if I were millions of times more pure and intelligent, I could not sufficiently extol you, for your glories are immeasurable. Nonetheless, I offer this with love—which also is a gift that you nurtured within us. So kindly accept it. Please uplift me and bestow upon me the qualification to finally be accepted as your eternal servant.

The foolish Bhakti Vikāsa Swami

2012

"That My Bubble May Not Burst"

Most dear, revered, incomprehensible, merciful Śrīla Prabhupāda:

Please accept my obeisance in the dust of your divine lotus feet.

In the book *Jaya Śrīla Prabhupāda!* (first published in 1994) I wrote about my "nonentity-ness": "Crowds do not run to greet me when I visit an ISKCON temple, nor do I have bundles of fan mail to neglect… whatever I do, good or bad, does not make much difference to anyone." Times have changed. Now I am an established ISKCON guru—albeit well behind the biggies, but enough of a celebrity to no longer have to travel by public bus, and to be greeted with *kīrtana* in many places (nice!), and yes, to have plenty of emails (from disciples and others) that I try to keep up with.

Within ISKCON, the role of guru is the most challenging and challenged institution. Now that I have come to this razor's edge, I pray that you maintain me in your service and protect me so that pride and complacency not spoil all that I am doing. Among the many servants of yours who are considerably more qualified than I, several have buckled under the strain of accepting disciples. My only hope for remaining fixed in this service is to constantly remember that despite being considered a dispenser of mercy, I am in every respect dependent on your mercy, and no less so than when I first came to the shelter of your lotus feet. Please grant me the sanity to play my part in pushing forward your mission, with full energy and with full confidence in your protection, and with the understanding that I am not and can never be anything but fully dependent on your mercy.

Śrīla Prabhupāda! I am still trying to come to grips with the paradox of being a guru, a spiritual master. How can a devotee, who is supposed to be the servant of everyone, be the master of anyone? Because you are a topmost devotee, you made it seem most natural to be simultaneously a servant and the spiritual master of the whole universe. You repeatedly stated that to be a guru is easy, yet you set a most difficult standard to emulate. To be a guru like you is not easy. Many facets of your divine personality—for instance, your natural charm and humility, and your defiance of physical laws such as those governing jetlag—seem far beyond my ability to emulate or even imitate. It is more realistic for me to try within my capacity to follow your example of selfless dedication to the *saṅkīrtana* mission.

Śrīla Prabhupāda, my disciples annually celebrate a function to honor me, which they call Vyāsa-*pūjā*. I trust that you are satisfied with that, for you have stated: "My glory will be when my disciples are worshiped all over the world."[49] Yet there is a clear distinction between Vyāsa-*pūjā* in my honor and Vyāsa-

pūjā in honor of Your Divine Grace. You are praised for being the great *mahā-bhāgavata* who, by representing the previous *ācāryas* and by your own extraordinary transcendental qualities, performed incomparable acts in spreading Kṛṣṇa consciousness throughout the world. On the other hand, the only praise that might be appropriate for me is that of being your faithful follower. To be a true follower of Your Divine Grace is no small thing, yet there will always be a gulf between you, the singular *mahā-bhāgavata* who widely distributed authentic love of Kṛṣṇa, and your many followers who—according to their realization, based on what they have heard from you (*yathā-mati yathā-śrutam*[50]) attempt to follow your example.

Śrīla Prabhupāda, because you are the mighty *mahā-bhāgavata* who founded ISKCON, to be your directly initiated disciple is a position of status in ISKCON today. Any "Prabhupāda disciple," even if deviated from his initiation vows and diverged from your teachings, is honored by juniors as a senior citizen of ISKCON—which is appropriate, for any cultured society respects its elders. Whatever else those disciples of yours may or may not have done throughout subsequent years, the struggles that they undertook for establishing Kṛṣṇa consciousness in the modern world should not be forgotten.

Nonetheless, to be a disciple of Your Divine Grace means more than being a relic or a mascot, more than merely socializing and reminiscing. Respect is accorded due to one's connection with you, but a living connection means to strive to live and act as you did. Śrīla Prabhupāda, you wanted your disciples to to be gurus, spiritual leaders of mankind, and in pursuance of your own unprecedented activities, to further vigorously promote the *saṅkīrtana* movement. You refused to fade away in old age, instead taking the freedom it afforded to go out into the world. You were not content to accept the honor accorded to elderly sadhus, but ventured among heathens and hippies. By personifying *amāninā mānadena*, you turned such dishonorable people into sadhus who now are worthy of the highest regard. You gave us everything—the real thing—and simply asked that we likewise give it to others.

Śrīla Prabhupāda, please take me beyond formality and grant me the privilege to follow in your footsteps. Let me not merely splutter and snuff out—another candle that could have given more light but simply faded away with the rest. Nor let my goal be merely to be remembered, or to create mythology meant to be perpetuated, or to playact as an icon who might seem genuine to those who have not actually heard your message. Śrīla Prabhupāda, please protect me from my wicked mind, which is ever prone to indulge in cheating. I want to be true to you and to others and not fail either you or the devotees of ISKCON, who are so dear to you.

One quality of a pure devotee is to be *apramattā* (not crazy).[51] Śrīla Prabhupāda, you are the only person whom I completely trust to be sane in all respects. Fully sane means fully free from even the subtlest of material desires. I am still insane—deeply insane. My only hope for sanity is to follow your instructions.

ācāryera mata yei sei mata sāra
tāṅra ājñā laṅghi 'cale sei ta 'asāra

> The order of the spiritual master is the active principle in spiritual life. Anyone who disobeys the order of the spiritual master immediately becomes useless.[52]

Śrīla Prabhupāda, during my very first days in your ISKCON, I imbibed this principle, and it has sustained me in your service throughout all of these years—to simply do what you have told us to do, with full trust that you are the intimate representative of Kṛṣṇa who is fully empowered by Him to deliver the entire world to His lotus feet. You are the master and we the servants, and we have no other duty than to obey your command. As we practically experience, all spiritual strength, all success,

follow from this principle. The essence of your instructions is to practice Kṛṣṇa consciousness seriously and propagate it vigorously. Please bless me that, despite the madness of my mind, I always adhere to this simple formula.

Śrīla Prabhupāda! *māyā,* in her typically inverse manner, is worshiping you by increasingly revealing your identity as the founder-*ācārya* of ISKCON. By demonstrating the perils of not adhering to your instructions, *māyā* helps convince us that all your plans are perfect and that to be an *ācārya* in your service means to serve your order; attempts to do otherwise simply result in disaster. We await the day when, as a movement, we will awaken from the collective amnesia of forgetting that all success is guaranteed if we simply stick to the simple principle of simply following your instructions.

In the meantime, the global insanity level is ever increasing, and only thanks to you can we still ascertain what is sane and what is not. Amid the insanity, we ever more deeply take shelter of your books, which truly are the only solace from the madness of this Kali-yuga. While associating with devotees who continue to follow your instructions (fortunately, within ISKCON there are still many such devotees), we marvel at how some of those who are meant to convey the teachings in your books seem to have never read them.

Śrīla Prabhupāda! Please grant me and all your aspiring followers the intelligence to understand that, although subsequent to your departure our knowledge and awareness of the extensive Vaiṣṇava culture and literature has inevitably increased, there will never be any question of "going beyond" what you have given us. It is you who are saving us all, and you live forever in your books. Please awaken in us the realization that in your books you have presented everything we need to know for becoming fully Kṛṣṇa conscious.

Śrīla Prabhupāda, your dear Lord Kṛṣṇa has kindly awarded me both a body and a personality that are not very attractive to women, and throughout all these years you have saved me from my lower bestial nature and protected me from gross capitulation to the charms of Cupid. Now that by default I am a little bigshot in ISKCON, *māyā* is offering me enhanced opportunities for self-infatuation, in the form of certain disciples and others seeming to regard me as something that I am not. To consider myself anything other than simply an aspiring servant in your service would certainly be a great disservice to one and all, and a major obstacle in my attempted service to you. Therefore I pray that you again save me.

Śrīla Prabhupāda, I never liked pettiness. I have always seen everyone around me as absorbed in petty concerns, and even their pressing issues as being mere trivia. I did not want that, and yearned for something better. I nearly despaired, but then I found you (or rather, you most mercifully found me). I will forsake crores of gross materialists and even scores of sadhus who do not, as did you, clearly and emphatically emphasize surrender to Kṛṣṇa, the Supreme Personality of Godhead. At least for me, you are the standard by which sadhus are to be judged; they are genuine to the extent that they reflect your character, qualities, and commitment to preaching Kṛṣṇa consciousness "as it is." They hold no appeal for me if they are significantly different to you. I want to associate with you, serve you, and be like you.

Śrīla Prabhupāda, to be your disciple means to ever aspire for the intense, unalloyed dedication to Kṛṣṇa that you personified and preached. I pray to live by and for the compelling spiritual truths that you incessantly delineated, and to not substitute them with a mere semblance of the vital Kṛṣṇa consciousness that you have given. May I ever cling to what I hear from you, and not be compromised by social niceties or supposed institutional necessities. Please award me the courage to truly represent you as I should, even if the whole world (including many who consider themselves yours) berate me for doing so. May I be ever unpopular if that is the price for clearly repeating the message that I so clearly hear from you. I deem this to be the true standard of a disciple, yet it is not easy to attain.

Śrīla Prabhupāda, although profoundly respecting all previous *ācāryas*, I know that my connection with Kṛṣṇa is primarily through you. Reading various writings of and about our previous *ācāryas* has enhanced not only my knowledge of and appreciation for our *sampradāya* and its gifts, but also my awareness that you are the most illustrious representative of the *sampradāya*, having been sent by Kṛṣṇa and the previous *ācāryas* to expertly present their message in a manner just suitable for the unique circumstances in which you preached Kṛṣṇa consciousness. Moreover, it was particularly Your Divine Grace who saved me.

brahmāṇḍa bhramite kona bhāgyavān jīva
guru-kṛṣṇa-prasāde pāya bhakti-latā-bīja[53]

Kṛṣṇa oversees each *jīva's* wanderings throughout the material universes, and for the most fortunate He ordains that at a certain point they meet a bona fide guru. And Kṛṣṇa arranged that I meet you, not any other of the exalted devotees who have come to this world to uplift fallen *jīvas*. It is Kṛṣṇa's desire, and my eternal good fortune, that I be linked especially with you.

Śrīla Prabhupāda, I gauge my spiritual standing according to my relationship with you, according to how much I remember that your mercy, which is attainable by following your orders, is the active principle in my life. Knowing that I am dependent on you, I pray for your mercy, feel grateful, and want to act as your humble servant. Everything else—my advancement in (or lack of) Kṛṣṇa consciousness and my various preaching endeavors—follows from that principle. Without remembering that your mercy is all that I am made of, then whatever I do, however much others might laud it, is just a sham.

Śrīla Prabhupāda, I need to keep your shoes upon my head. My only proper and safe position is at your feet. But I cannot fully avail the shelter of your shoes if I retain interest in sense gratification in any form or have any inclination toward *māyāvāda*. Please purify me by immersing me in your service. Just as you saved me so many years ago from intense distress by accepting me, please now save me from comfort and delusion and again make me your disciple. In the dust of your lotus feet and aspiring to be the servant of your servants,

the very fallen Bhakti Vikāsa Swami

2013

nama oṁ viṣṇu-pādāya kṛṣṇa-preṣṭhāya bhū-tale
śrīmate bhaktivedānta-svāminn iti nāmine
namas te sārasvate deve gaura-vāṇī-pracāriṇe
nirviśeṣa-śūnyavādi-pāścātya-deśa-tāriṇe

Śrīla Prabhupāda, recently a Śrī Vaiṣṇava *ācārya* invited me to a *thirumañjanam* (elaborate ceremony of worship) of Śrī Rāmānujācārya. That was another occasion for me to observe how the *sampradāya* to which Śrī Rāmānujācārya gave new life, meaning, and direction is still united around him many hundreds of years after the period of his manifest activities.

About three hundred years after Śrī Rāmānuja's withdrawal from manifest activities, his *sampradāya* split doctrinally into two warring camps, each of which quite differently interpreted certain teachings of his. Even today both sects continue, their previous acrimony and doctrinal differences largely overlooked or forgotten. The very reason for the longevity of both divisions has been their sworn adherence to Śrī Rāmānuja's teachings, regarding both *siddhānta* and practice.

The long-standing coherence of the Mādhva-sampradāya must also be principally ascribed to the fact that its members are loyal to the teachings of their founding-*ācārya*.

Similarly, in your ISKCON, strength derives from adherence to the teachings of the founder-*ācārya*, namely Your Divine Grace.

Śrīla Prabhupāda, although those teachings are available to all, and although to be your follower plainly means to follow your teachings, nowadays there are multiple interpretations of several of those teachings, and devotees who claim to be your followers are divided on various issues. Some camps have already sprung up outside the ambit of the ISKCON that you incorporated, and presently some doctrinal disagreements threaten to sunder the core movement that you established.

In this predicament, it is particularly apt to recall the following statements from your teachings:

keha ta 'ācārya ājñāya keha ta 'svatantra
sva-mata kalpanā kare daiva-paratantra

> [Translation:] Some of the disciples strictly accepted the orders of the *ācārya*, and others deviated, independently concocting their own opinions under the spell of *daivī-māyā*.
>
> [Purport:] This verse describes the beginning of a schism. When disciples do not stick to the principle of accepting the order of their spiritual master, immediately there are two opinions. Any opinion different from the opinion of the spiritual master is useless. One cannot infiltrate materially concocted ideas into spiritual advancement. That is deviation. There is no scope for adjusting spiritual advancement to material ideas. [*Caitanya-caritāmṛta, Ādi* 12.9]

ācāryera mata yei sei mata sāra
tāṅra ājñā laṅghi 'cale sei ta 'asāra

[Translation:] The order of the spiritual master is the active principle in spiritual life. Anyone who disobeys the order of the spiritual master immediately becomes useless.

[Purport:] Here is the opinion of Śrīla Kṛṣṇadāsa Kavirāja Gosvāmī. Persons who strictly follow the orders of the spiritual master are useful in executing the will of the Supreme, whereas persons who deviate from the strict order of the spiritual master are useless. [*Caitanya-caritāmṛta, Ādi* 12. 10]

* * *

There are many disciples of Bhaktisiddhānta Sarasvatī Ṭhākura, but to judge who is actually his disciple, to divide the useful from the useless, one must measure the activities of such disciples in executing the will of the spiritual master.... [B]y accepting the criterion recommended by Kṛṣṇadāsa Kavirāja Gosvāmī, one can very easily understand who is a genuine world-preacher and who is useless. [*Caitanya-caritāmṛta, Ādi* 12.12, purport]

* * *

If the Absolute Truth is one, about which we think there is no difference of opinion, the guru also cannot be two. The Ācāryadeva for whom we have assembled tonight to offer our humble homage is not the guru of a sectarian institution or one out of many differing exponents of the truth. On the contrary, he is the *jagad-guru,* or the guru of all of us. The only difference is that some obey him wholeheartedly, while others do not obey him directly. [From your speech on the occasion of the Vyāsa-*pūjā* of Śrīla Bhaktisiddhānta Sarasvatī Gosvāmī, February 1936]

* * *

The main business of human society is to think of the Supreme Personality of Godhead at all times, to become His devotees, to worship the Supreme Lord, and to bow down before Him. The *ācārya,* the authorized representative of the Supreme

> Lord, establishes these principles, but when he disappears, things once again become disordered. The perfect disciples of the *ācārya* try to relieve the situation by sincerely following the instructions of the spiritual master. [*Śrīmad-Bhāgavatam* 4.28.48, purport]

Śrīla Prabhupāda, I pray that you may count me among those disciples of yours who are sincerely following your instructions. Please bless me with the association of those whom you have blessed with the unsullied vision and determination to always sincerely and wholeheartedly obey your instructions. Please protect me from the association and influence of persons who profess to be your followers yet do not obey you directly—for instance, by not rising early every day for *sādhana*, or by preaching and teaching in a manner distinctly different from yours.

You told us to be *śāstra-cakṣuḥ*. Accordingly, a sincere disciple will always try to understand everything through the instructions in your books. By reading your books one can clearly observe that the principle of *anyābhilāṣitā-śūnya*—which is the central pulse of your teachings—is nowadays considerably compromised within the society that you founded for establishing this principle within the world. Hence, much of what passes as being adherent to your instructions is in fact a deviation from them.

Quoting again from your purport to *Śrīmad-Bhāgavatam* 4.28.48:

> The perfect disciples of the *ācārya* try to relieve the situation by sincerely following the instructions of the spiritual master. At the present moment practically the entire world is afraid of rogues and nondevotees; therefore this Kṛṣṇa consciousness movement is started to save the world from irreligious principles. Everyone should cooperate with this movement in order to bring about actual peace and happiness in the world.

Śrīla Prabhupāda, you are the most important *ācārya* in this Kali-yuga, and your instructions, if perfectly understood and executed, can effect tremendous good for the entire universe—as is recognized even by leaders of other Vaiṣṇava *sampradāyas*. For instance, during a public meeting several years ago Śrī Viśveśvara Tīrtha, a widely revered patriarch of the Mādhva-sampradāya, stated, "ISKCON is the only organization that can spread *viṣṇu-bhakti* throughout the world."

It could be said that the very cause of the longevity of the old Vaiṣṇava *sampradāyas* is also the cause of their present admitted inability to spread *viṣṇu-bhakti* throughout the world. Ācāryas Rāmānuja and Madhva are fully worshipable by us, as are their teachings and the followers of their teachings. But, as ordained by Lord Caitanya, now is the time for *gaura-vāṇī* to spread widely via the personage of Your Divine Grace. As the Śrī Vaiṣṇava *ācārya* whom I mentioned above told me, in his *sampradāya* there are many elaborate procedures, but you made *bhakti* easily available to all.

Śrīla Prabhupāda, one of the reasons that you were able to spread Kṛṣṇa consciousness worldwide was your ability to present "old wine in new bottles." You knew the art of maintaining basic principles while adjusting details according to time, place, and circumstance. Yet we who claim to be your followers must be careful to not imitate (*anukaraṇa*) your example rather than faithfully following in your footsteps (*anusaraṇa*). If, due to inexpertness in distinguishing details from principles, we infiltrate materially concocted ideas into spiritual advancement (in the name of "time, place, and circumstance"), and in so doing fail to bring about the revolution of *bhakti* that you envisioned, then we shall surely be *asāra*.

What must we do to save ourselves from the same accusations that you leveled at your godbrothers? For the answer, we must look within your teachings—which you gave to us minute by minute during your manifest presence, and continue to give us through your books—and we must be sufficiently sincere to wholeheartedly accept those teachings unchanged and in toto. We must beseech you for the discrimination by which to distinguish details from principles, and for the empowerment to dynamically continue the *paramparā* without becoming either anachronisms or rank speculators.

Your teachings are as clear and brilliant as the sun, yet great harm can be done if persons who present themselves as teachers of your teachings instead attempt to mix or replace them with their own materially infiltrated concoctions. If you see fit, please bless me to serve your mission during this critical period by careful, prayerful study of your pristine message, and with the ability to delineate it via both the spoken and written word, particularly to distinguish it from various misrepresentations; and also bless me to not be just an armchair critic but to continue to be actively involved in your mission in multiple ways, giving special attention to two crucial programs that are presently nearly forgotten, namely *daiva-varṇāśrama* and *gurukula*.

Śrīla Prabhupāda, please give me the intelligence and wisdom to understand that, although you have given certain parameters the stepping outside of which disqualifies one as your genuine disciple, still there is no "one" way to be your follower. This is clear from your having accepted all kinds of people and encouraged them in various ways in your magnanimous, pragmatic endeavors to engage every *jīva* within the entire universe in Kṛṣṇa consciousness. Considering this, I must also bear in mind your instructions regarding your disciples' cooperating together, unity in diversity, the story of the quarreling sons beating their father rather than massaging him, excessive and inappropriate liberality in devotional service (*niyama-agraha*) vs. fanaticism (*niyama-āgraha*), plus your own example of repeatedly trying to work with your godbrothers (despite their indifference toward such proposals) yet also castigating them, and of course Śrī Caitanya Mahāprabhu's essential *tṛṇād api* call for humility and tolerance—notwithstanding that all of these dictums are commonly misinterpreted and misapplied.

Always seeking your mercy, without which I have no hope of any good fortune—what to speak of executing any grandiose plans—I pray to always be

Your dedicated servant,

Bhakti Vikāsa Swami

2014

Śrīla Prabhupāda, you are the glorious, incomparable *paramahaṁsa* whose preaching in the Western world was the only thing of any real importance that ever happened there.

Of course, Vyāsa-*pūjā* offerings are meant for glorifying the guru as the representative and worshiper of Vyāsa. Yet we have learned from you that in the physical absence of the guru, he may be best worshiped by the continuation of his mission. As you pointed out in your 1961 Vyāsa-*pūjā* offering to your own guru-mahārāja, a festival of flowers and fruits is not the real *pūjā;* rather, one who serves the guru's message truly worships him.

Śrīla Prabhupāda, in your 1958 "Viraha-aṣṭāṣṭaka" submission to your guru-māhāraja, you expressed deep dissatisfaction upon observing the disorientation of his mission:

> That your ocean of compassion has again become dammed is to me a great spear piercing my heart.

More of your reflections therein are:

> Those devotees to whom the responsibility was given to continue spreading this flood of love somehow became overpowered by Māyā.
>
> Without Caitanya Mahāprabhu's message being spread there is only confusion and upheaval in the movement.
>
> The tigress of ambition has appeared within your mission, which is conducted by devotees who are irresolute in devotional service. The mission has expanded, but with many factions.
>
> The essential purport of your message did not enter their ears.
>
> Where are your instructions still being followed?

Many of these statements concerning the mission of your guru bear obvious similarities to the situation within your own institution today, and thus we can begin to comprehend some of the distress that you must again be experiencing on seeing the present state of your ISKCON.

In the following quotes, "you," in reference to your gurudeva, could well be reapplied to ourselves in reference to Your Divine Grace:

> If, at such a time as this, you were to return to this world and once more preach in the same manner that you always did, if again there were such kind of preaching in every direction, then, as before, everyone would be stirred up in bliss.
>
> Your deep roaring would make the demons and atheists flee, and your narrations of Lord Caitanya's message would fill the *jīvas'* hearts.
>
> If you were to again come, then again the whole world would be dynamized.

Śrīla Prabhupāda, it has been 118 years since you mercifully appeared in this world, and 37 years since Kṛṣṇa called you back to Him. At the time of your departure, your disciples clearly understood your mandate and were confident that if we simply adhered to your instructions, amazing things would continue to unfold as they had throughout your manifest presence, and very soon Kṛṣṇa consciousness would overtake the world.

Obviously, all has not happened as expected. Although the Kṛṣṇa consciousness movement has much increased since 1977, no one who was then present and is not amnesic or delusional would deny that much of what is mainstream in ISKCON today would at that time have been considered an unthinkable deviation from your instructions and example. There is no need to elaborate on this herein. I am but one among many (including mundane scholars) who have commented about the ongoing redefinition of what is meant to be your ISKCON. Some devotees call this mission drift, but I see it more as a hijack.

Śrīla Prabhupāda, I just need to let you know that I am not aligned with persons who use your name and institution to promote their own agenda, among which some programs bear hardly even a semblance to your mission. I unequivocally accept you as the founder-*ācārya* of ISKCON and I aspire to associate with those devotees whose resolve is to serve your ISKCON, not some other version.

Śrīla Prabhupāda, I am often reminded that you strongly desired that all of your disciples cooperate. But it is mere sophistry to substitute your pristine directions with one's own concoctions and then, in your name, demand cooperation.

Śrīla Prabhupāda, you gave substance to my miserable and empty life. Please again save me from darkness and grant me the association of your genuine followers.

The lowly

Bhakti Vikāsa Swami

Acknowledgements

My thanks to everyone who helped produce this second edition, prominent among whom were:

Editing—Guru-Kṛṣṇa Dāsa

Layout—Vṛndāvana-candra Dāsa

Proofreading—Kiśora Dāsa and Ananta-sarovara Dāsī, Indirā-sakhī Devī Dāsī, Murāri Dāsa, Prāṇa-vallabhī Devī Dāsī, Śrīdhara Śrīnivāsa Dāsa, Śrī Giridhārī Dāsa

Cover design—Mādhava Dāsa

Printing supervision—Śrī Giridhārī Dāsa

About Bhakti Vikāsa Swami

The author was born in Britain in 1957 and joined ISKCON in London in 1975. Later that year, he was formally accepted as a disciple of His Divine Grace A. C. Bhaktivedanta Swami Prabhupāda, the founder-*ācārya* of ISKCON, and renamed Ilāpati Dāsa.

From 1977 to 1979 Ilāpati Dāsa was based in India, mainly distributing Śrīla Prabhupāda's books throughout West Bengal. In the following ten years, he helped pioneer ISKCON activities in Bangladesh, Malaysia, Myanmar, and Thailand.

In 1989 Ilāpati Dāsa accepted the order of *sannyāsa,* receiving the name Bhakti Vikāsa Swami, and again made his base in India. Since then he has been preaching Kṛṣṇa consciousness mostly throughout the subcontinent—lecturing in English, Hindi, and Bengali—but also for a few months each year in other parts of the world. His television lectures in Hindi have reached millions worldwide.

Bhakti Vikāsa Swami writes extensively on Kṛṣṇa conscious topics. His books have been translated into over twenty languages, with over a million in print.

Notes

References

The words *Conversation*, *Lecture*, *Letter*, and *Purport* indicate quotations taken from published editions by or involving Śrīla Prabhupāda.

1 Lecture, 5 May 1976.
2 Letter, 14 Oct 1973.
3 Letters of 16 Jun 1969, 20 Aug 1974, and 22 Nov 1974.
4 Letter, 12 Mar 1977.
5 Lecture, 6 Sep 1976.
6 Conversation, 9 Oct 1975.
7 SB 3.32.3, purport.
8 *Nectar of Devotion*, ch. 10.
9 SB 4.12.27, purport.
10 My *Glorious Master* (by Bhūrijana Dāsa) pp. 258–59.
11 See Cc *Ādi* 7.95.
12 *ISKCON in the 1970s* (by Satsvarūpa Dāsa Goswami) vol. 1, p. 70 (lightly edited).
13 Conversation, 27–29 Feb 1972.
14 Letter, 4 Sep 1972.
15 Lecture, 8 Feb 1977.
16 A *Transcendental Diary* (by Hari Śauri Dāsa), vol. 4, page xi.
17 Letter, 20 Feb 1969.
18 *TKG's Diary*, May 23.
19 Letter, 2 Jan 1971.
20 Cc *Madhya* 4.79, purport.
21 Lecture, 6 Sep 1976.
22 SB 5.5.2.
23 Conversation, 22 Apr 1974.
24 Conversation, 10 Jan 1974.
25 Lecture, 15 Jul 1975.

26 *Śrīla Prabhupāda-līlāmṛta*, ch. 50, "The Lame Man and the Blind Man."

27 Conversation, 27 May 1977.

28 SB, Śrīla Prabhupāda's Dedication.

29 Letter, 19 Sep 1974.

30 Letter, 16 Jan 1975.

31 Letter, 1 Feb 1975.

32 Although this is a fairly well-known anecdote, a reference for it has not been found.

33 Letter, 1 Apr 1974.

34 Letter, 28 Dec 1974.

35 Lecture, 2 Mar 1975.

36 Letter, 7 Oct 1974.

37 *ISKCON in the 1970's*, vol. 1, p. 77.

38 *Caitanya-śikṣāmṛta* 3.2.

39 *Bhagavad-gītā* 18.69.

40 Personal recollection by Svavaśa Dāsa.

41 *Śrīla Prabhupāda-līlāmṛta*, ch. 26, "Swamiji's Departure."

42 Lecture, 7 Feb 1969.

43 Personal recollection by Pṛthu Dāsa.

44 SB 10.80.41.

45 Lecture, 4 Mar 1975.

46 Letter, 9 Aug 1976.

47 Letter, 29 Jul 1976.

48 Letter, 14 Aug 1976.

49 Told by Bhakta Dāsa Prabhu; Śrīla Prabhupāda Tributes 2011, p. 153.

50 SB 3.6.36.

51 Cc *Madhya* 22.80.

52 Cc *Ādi* 12.10.

53 Cc. *Madhya* 19.151.

Other Books by Bhakti Vikāsa Swami

A Beginner's Guide to Kṛṣṇa Consciousness

Read this book and improve your life!

All you need to know to get started in Kṛṣṇa consciousness. Easy-to-understand guidance on daily practices that bring us closer to Kṛṣṇa. Packed with practical information. Suitable both for devotees living in an ashram or at home.

Guaranteed to make you a better, more spiritual person

120 x 180 mm • 132 pages • line art • softbound

Available also in Bengali, Croatian, Gujarati, Hindi, Indonesian, Kannada, Malayalam, Marathi, Nepali, Polish, Russian, Slovene, Tamil, Telugu, and Urdu

A Message to the Youth of India

Youth of India, Awake!

Your country is destined to lead the world by spiritual strength. Understand the power of your own culture, which is attracting millions from all over the world.

Religion, philosophy, social and historical analysis. Compelling insights, not only for the youth but for all interested in the future of India and the world.

Arise, come forward, be enlightened

120 x 180 mm • 128 pages • softbound

Available also in Bengali, Gujarati, Hindi, Marathi, Tamil, and Telugu

Brahmacarya in Kṛṣṇa Consciousness

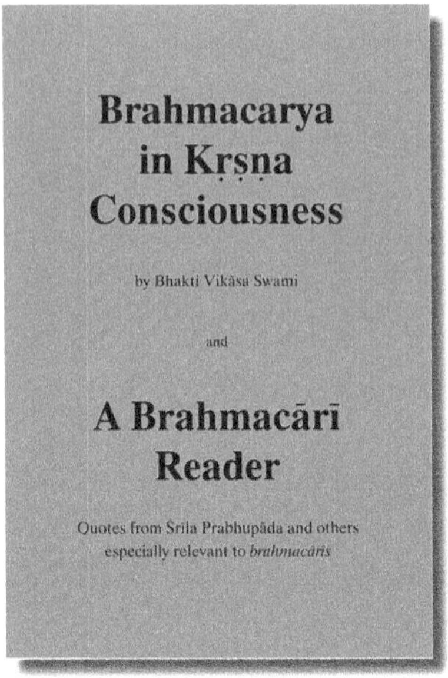

A "user's guide" to *brahmacārī* life. The first part consists of elaborate discussions and practical guidance regarding many aspects of *brahmacarya.* The second portion is a compilation of quotations on *brahmacarya* from Śrīla Prabhupāda's books, letters, and recordings.

Invaluable not only for *brahmacārīs* but for all devotees seriously interested in improving their spiritual life.

135 x 210 mm • 272 pages • softbound

Available also in Bengali, Croatian, Gujarati, Hindi, Indonesian, Italian, Mandarin, Portuguese, Russian, and Tamil

Glimpses of Traditional Indian Life

Journey to the real India. Discover the wisdom and devotion at the heart of Indian life. Meet people who were raised in a godly atmosphere and learn how it shaped their character and enriched their life. Explore the adverse effects of India's technological development, the downfall of her hereditary culture, and other causes of India's present degradation.

135 x 210 mm • 256 pages • 16 color plates • softbound

Available also in Croatian and Russian

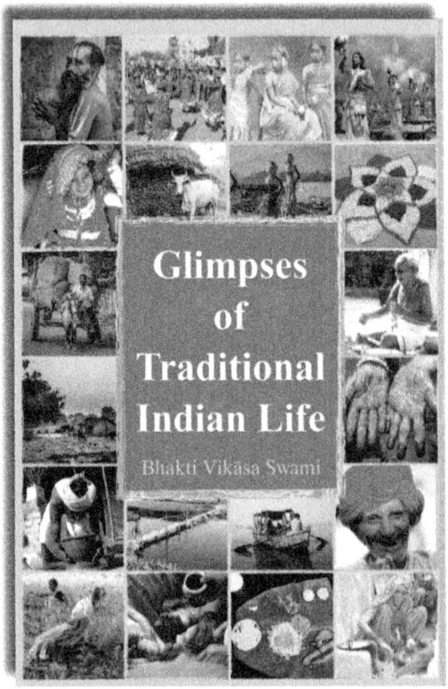

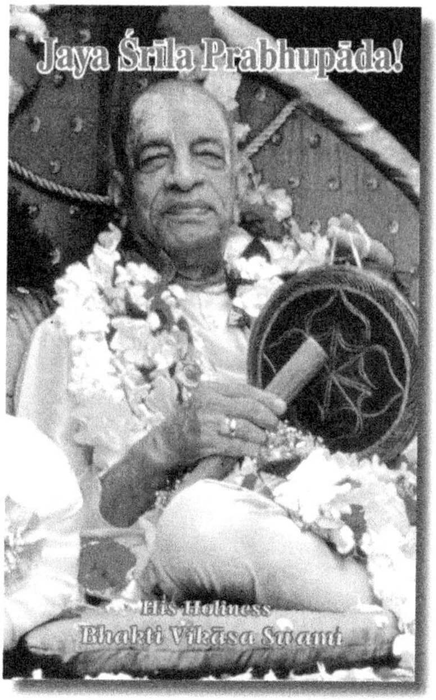

Jaya Śrīla Prabhupāda!

There is no limit to Śrīla Prabhupāda's transcendental attributes, nor do we wish to ever stop describing them. His qualities, combined with his achievements, undoubtedly establish Śrīla Prabhupāda as an extraordinarily great transcendental personality.

Śrīla Prabhupāda is still with us, watching over the continuing expansion of the Kṛṣṇa consciousness movement. If we simply follow his instructions carefully, we can expect many amazing, unimaginable things to happen.

135 x 210 mm • 240 pages • pictures and line art • softbound

Available also in Gujarati, Russian, and Tamil

The Story of Rasikānanda

Śrī Rasikānanda Deva was a mighty Vaiṣṇava *ācārya* in the era after Lord Caitanya's disappearance. Along with his guru, Śrīla Śyāmānanda Paṇḍita, he inundated North Orissa and surrounding districts in waves of Kṛṣṇa-*prema* that are still flowing today. He subdued and converted atheists, blasphemers, and dacoits, and even tamed and initiated a rogue elephant! The exciting story of Śrī Rasikānanda Deva is told herein.

135 x 210 mm • 216 pages • 4 color plates • softbound

Available also in Gujarati, and Russian

On Pilgrimage in Holy India

Travel with an ISKCON sannyasi, including to some of India's less-known but most charming holy places.

210 x 280 mm • 196 pages • full-color with 191 pictures • hardbound

Available also in Russian

Rāmāyaṇa

Countless eons ago, when men and animals could converse together and powerful *brāhmaṇas* would effect miracles, the uncontrollable demon Rāvaṇa was terrorizing the universe. The *Rāmāyaṇa* records the adventures of Rāma, the Lord of righteousness, as He struggles to overcome the forces of Rāvaṇa. This absorbing narration has delighted and enlightened countless generations in India, and its timeless spiritual insights are compellingly relevant in today's confused world.

135 x 210 mm • 600 pages • 16 color plates • line art • hardbound

Available also in Croatian, Gujarati, Hindi, Latvian, Marathi, Polish, Russian, Telugu, and Thai

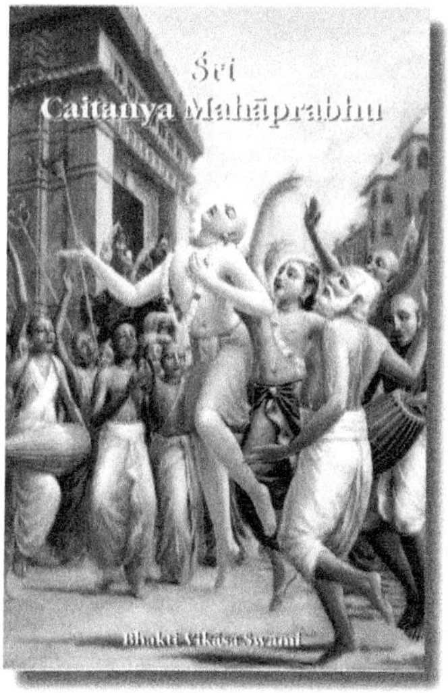

Śrī Caitanya Mahāprabhu

Hundreds of thousands of people throughout the world now follow the spotless path of Kṛṣṇa consciousness as given by Lord Caitanya. Chanting the holy names of Kṛṣṇa and dancing in ecstasy, they desire only love of Kṛṣṇa and consider material enjoyment to be insignificant. This book gives an overview of the life and teachings of Śrī Caitanya Mahāprabhu, the most munificent avatar ever to grace this planet.

120 x 180 mm • 176 pages • 16 color plates • softbound

Available also in Gujarati, Hindi, Russian, Tamil, and Telugu

Śrī Vaṁśīdāsa Bābājī

Śrīla Vaṁsīdāsa Bābājī was a great Vaiṣṇava who although physically present in this world, had little communication with it. His hair and beard were uncut, matted, and dishevelled. He almost never bathed, and his eyes looked wild. He wore only a loin cloth, and nothing more.

This book introduces us to a personality of such extraordinary, inscrutable character that we simply offer him obeisance and beg for his mercy.

135 x 210 mm • 152 pages
• 8 color plates • softbound

Available also in Croatian, Hindi, and Russian

Women: Masters or Mothers?

Women: Masters or Mothers? presents traditionalist arguments for the direction of the Kṛṣṇa consciousness movement, proposing that we should take up Śrīla Prabhupāda's mandate to establish *varṇāśrama-dharma* rather than capitulate to the norms and ideologies of secular culture. Particularly discussed are gender roles, parental responsibilities, feminist follies, and some of Śrīla Prabhupāda's more controversial teachings, such as those concerning early marriage, divorce, and polygamy.

140 x 216 mm • 216 pages • paperback • 150 Lectures DVD

Available in English

Śrī Bhaktisiddhānta Vaibhava

Śrīla Bhaktisiddhānta Sarasvatī Ṭhākura altered the course of religious history by reviving and forcefully propagating pure Kṛṣṇa consciousness. His boldness in combating cheating religion earned him the appellation "lion guru"—yet his heart was soft with divine love for Kṛṣṇa.

Based in Bengal and traveling throughout India in the early twentieth century, Śrīla Bhaktisiddhānta Sarasvatī Ṭhākura laid the foundation for, and was the inspiration and guiding force behind, the later worldwide spreading of the Hare Kṛṣṇa movement.

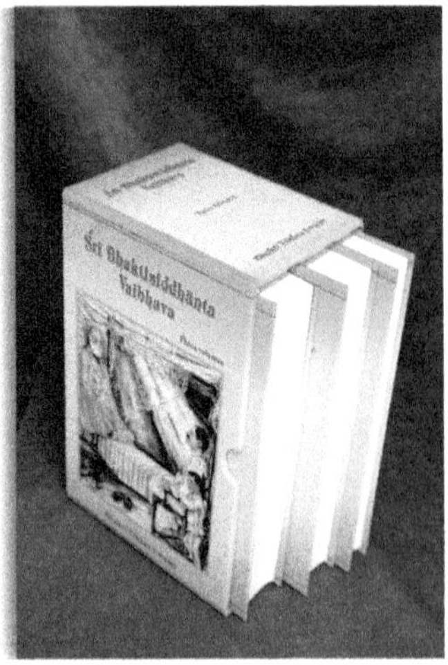

The result of over twenty years of research, *Śrī Bhaktisiddhānta Vaibhava* presents a wealth of newly translated material. Replete with anecdotes told by disciples who lived with him, this devotional, philosophical, cultural, and historical study gives intimate insights into the activities, teachings, and character of an empowered emissary of the Supreme Lord.

160 x 240 mm • 1576 pages • 164 black-and-white photos • 9 color photos • hardbound • decorative protective box

Śrī Bhaktisiddhānta Vaibhava is presented in three volumes

Volume 1 features a biographical overview, plus detailed analysis of the message, mission, and personality of Śrīla Bhaktisiddhānta Sarasvati.

Volume 2 details the preaching challenge that Śrīla Bhaktisiddhānta Sarasvati faced, and also includes biographical sketches of several of his disciples and associates.

Volume 3 features an overview of Śrīla Bhaktisiddhānta Sarasvati's contributions, with selections from his lectures, writings, and colloquies, also his astrological chart, and appendixes that include important details concerning Śrīla Bhaktisiddhānta Sarasvati and the Gauḍīya Maṭha.

On Speaking Strongly in Śrīla Prabhupāda's Service

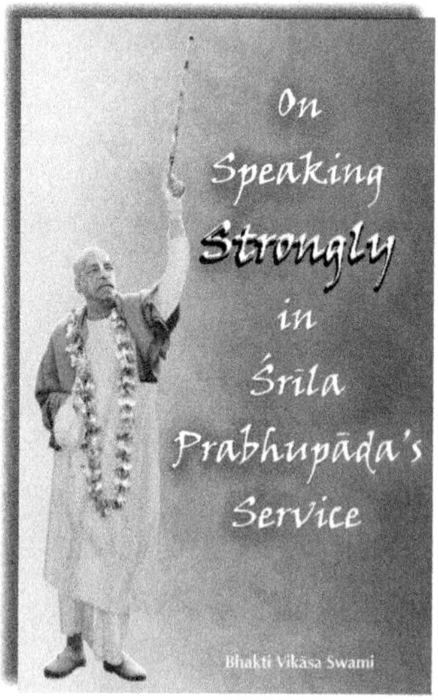

Why followers of Śrīla Prabhupāda should speak strongly, as he did. A comprehensive analysis of how to present Kṛṣṇa consciousness straightforwardly, intelligently, and effectively. Features many anecdotes and more than five hundred powerful quotes.

135 x 210 mm • 272 pages
• hardbound • multimedia CD

For more information, please visit:
www.speakingstrongly.com

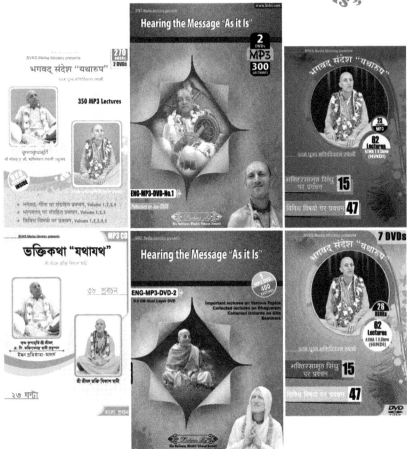